JOY RISING

Boundaries, Bravery, and a Bit of Bliss

CAROLYN PISTONE

ISBN: 979-8-9949121-0-2 (eBook)
ISBN: 979-8-9949121-1-9 (Paperback)
ISBN: 979-8-9949121-2-6 (Audiobook)

What People Are Saying About *Joy Rising*

Wise. Warm. Funny. Fierce. A book about choosing joy when it would be easier not to.

"Carolyn Pistone writes about joy the way some people write about survival—because for her, they are the same thing. This book is generous, irreverent, deeply compassionate, and exactly what I needed when I didn't know I needed it."

—Gena P., Author and speaker

"I laughed, I cried, I underlined entire pages. *Joy Rising* is not a self-help book—it's a permission slip. To feel pleasure. To set boundaries. To keep your sense of humor while the world is on fire."

—Karen C., Workshop participant

"This book reminded me that joy isn't naïve—it's defiant. Carolyn Pistone shows us that choosing joy is not escapism, it's courage. And sometimes, it's also just really funny."

—E.G., Community leader

"Reading *Joy Rising* felt like being lovingly called out and warmly hugged at the same time. Carolyn's voice is honest, witty, and deeply reassuring.

This is a book I'll return to again and again."

—Rick R., Executive and longtime reader of *Open for Joy*

Dedication

For Miguel and all the joy that was.
For Marty and all the joy that is and will be ‘til the end.
For Yuuki and all the joy that is, was,
and always will be, thanks
to you for lighting the way.

Table of Contents

Foreword

Joy Rising is not a book about pretending life is easy. It is a book about telling the truth and choosing joy anyway. I loved Carolyn's first book, but this book is by far my favorite. Why? The stories are vulnerable, raw, messy, and joyful. My attention was captive from the start!

As a clinician, I spend my days listening for what lives beneath the surface: the stories people carry in their bodies, the places where pain and meaning intersect, and the quiet ways resilience shows up long before anyone calls it strength. As a human, I know that insight alone is not enough. Healing has to meet real life. This book does exactly that.

Each chapter explores a place where joy is often misunderstood, dismissed, or withheld, and gently insists that joy still belongs there.

The early chapters invite us to reclaim joy through lived experience. Travel becomes perspective rather than escape. Sexuality is named as a birthright without bypassing trauma or shame. Suffering is not minimized, but joy is allowed to coexist with grief, fear, and loss. Clinically, this reflects what we know to be true: joy does not erase pain, but it does support survival and meaning-making.

As the book moves forward, joy is framed as a practice. Integrity at work, joy as protest, and connection to nature remind us that joy is not passive or indulgent. It is often a response to moral courage, presence, and alignment. These chapters reflect the psychological cost of disconnection and the healing power of living in accordance with one's values.

The later chapters ask us to see more clearly. They address privilege, faith, mortality, gaslighting, and the reclamation of self. These themes are both deeply personal and clinically significant. Joy cannot survive where reality is denied or where identity is erased. Reclaiming joy often begins with reclaiming truth.

The final chapters do not offer closure or easy answers. They offer hope as a practice and joy as something that continues to rise, even in uncertain times.

This is not a book that tells you how to be joyful.

It invites you to notice where joy is already trying to return.

As a clinician, I appreciate its honesty and emotional intelligence.

As a human, I appreciate its companionship.

This book does not demand joy.

It makes room for it.

And that, in itself, is healing.

Masterfully done, Carolyn! I am deeply honored to have written this Foreword and can't wait for your next book!

Fondly,
Karen Robinson, MSW, ACSW,
LCSW, CCTP-II
Trauma Recovery Expert

Preface

When I wrote *Open for Joy: A Journey of Healing and Business Success*, I was standing at the doorway.

I was a first-time author. I genuinely didn't know if what I had written even was a book. Maybe I still don't. I knew I had something to say, but I didn't yet trust the sound of my voice on the page. I pressed "send" with equal parts hope and terror and figured I'd let the world decide.

Then I went to record the audiobook.

Standing in a sound studio, reading my own words out loud, I kept having to stop myself from rewriting the book entirely. I wanted to add stories, clarify points, and say, "Oh wait—this part matters more than I realized." It took real discipline not to keep interrupting myself mid-sentence with, "Well actually..."

And that's when it hit me.

I wasn't finished.

I hadn't said everything I needed to say—not because the first book was incomplete, but because I was still unfolding. The stories were still arriving. The understanding was still deepening. The joy I had cracked open was asking to rise.

That realization—born in a quiet recording studio with a microphone and my own voice echoing back at me—is where Joy Rising began.

I had lived enough life to know that joy was real, powerful, and necessary—but I was still learning how to let it in. That book was an invitation. To myself, first. To notice joy. To allow it. To stop assuming it was frivolous or undeserved. To recognize that joy wasn't something that happened after the hard parts of life, but something that could exist alongside them.

I didn't know then how much further the conversation would need to go.

Since that book came into the world, life has continued to do what life does. It has delivered beauty and terror, love and loss, laughter and grief—often all at the same time. I've watched joy show up in places I never expected, and I've watched it be threatened, dismissed, politicized, and misunderstood. I've also come to see something I didn't fully grasp before:

Joy is not just personal.
It's relational.
It's political.
It's defiant.
And sometimes, it's downright rebellious.

This book is not about finding joy.

It's about choosing it.

Choosing joy when circumstances would prefer you numb, compliant, afraid, or small. Choosing joy when grief has a permanent seat at the table. Choosing joy in your body, your work, your relationships, your protests, your faith, your pleasure, your aging, and your mortality.

If *Open for Joy* was about opening the door, *Joy Rising* is about what happens when you step fully inside and refuse to leave—even when the world insists you do.

You won't find tidy answers here. You'll find stories. Stories of travel, sex, work, illness, injustice, and love. Stories of getting it wrong, laughing anyway, and trying again. Stories where joy doesn't erase suffering—but survives it. Sometimes even because of it.

I didn't write this book because I have joy figured out.
I wrote it because I've learned that joy is not a luxury.
It's not a reward.
And it's not optional.

Joy is a practice.

A birthright.

A responsibility.

And in times like these, choosing joy—out loud, in public, and with your whole heart—might just be one of the most radical things you can do.

If you haven't read *Open for Joy*, you're not late, behind, or missing anything essential. This book stands on its own. You don't need a résumé of healing, a business success story, or a perfectly curated life to be here. You just need curiosity—and maybe a willingness to laugh at yourself once in a while.

Joy Rising is not a sequel in the traditional sense. It's more of a continuation of a conversation that began when I stopped pretending I had everything figured out. It's for anyone who has survived something, built something, lost something, questioned everything—or all of the above, sometimes before breakfast.

This book is an invitation, not a prescription. An offering, not a performance. You won't find five easy steps or a tidy formula for happiness. Instead, you'll find stories—some joyful, some messy, some surprising—that point to a simple truth I keep relearning: joy doesn't wait for permission and doesn't require perfection.

So, wherever you're coming from—whether you're hopeful, skeptical, exhausted, curious, or just killing time in a bookstore aisle—I'm glad you're here. Take what resonates. Leave what doesn't. And if something in these pages makes you feel a little more alive, a little more seen, or a little more willing to rise into your own joy... then we're already doing this together.

I don't claim expertise—only experience. These are my stories, my reflections, and my best guesses about what they mean. If any of it helps you, even a little, then it's done its job.

The stories in this book are inspired by the author's life experiences and reflections. Some details and identifying characteristics have been changed to protect the privacy of individuals.

Introduction

This is not a book about pretending everything is fine. In fact, even as I write this introduction, I find myself in extremely trying times. Often, through gritted teeth, I grumble, "But I'm supposed to be an expert on Joy!" All of us are living through a life that constantly challenges and tests us.

It's not a book about positive thinking, manifesting parking spaces, or bypassing pain with platitudes. And it's definitely not about joy as some kind of moral obligation—another thing to get right or feel bad about getting wrong.

This is a book about joy as a *practice*.
A choice.
A reclaiming.

It's about joy that shows up alongside grief, fear, rage, humor, love, and very human messiness. The kind of joy that endures bad timing, broken systems, disappointing people, aging bodies, and moments when the world feels like it's spinning slightly off its axis.

The stories in this book are personal, but they're not precious. They're drawn from travel and work, love and loss, parenting and partnership, protest signs and hospital rooms, dance floors and boardrooms. Some are funny. Some are tender. Some still make me shake my head and say, *Well... that happened.*

What ties them together is this: Again and again, life offered me opportunities to shrink, harden, or disappear—and yet I kept stumbling back toward joy. Sometimes gracefully. Often not.

Occasionally, with excellent timing. More often with bruises and a sense of humor.

Joy Rising is not about arriving anywhere. It's about noticing what happens when you stop postponing joy until things are "resolved," "safe," or "appropriate." It's about what becomes possible when you decide that joy isn't the reward at the end of the road but part of the road itself.

You don't need to have read my first book to be here. You don't need to agree with me. You don't need to be healed, hopeful, or even particularly optimistic. All you need is a little curiosity—and maybe a willingness to laugh when things get awkward.

My only real invitation is this:
As you read, notice where joy is already trying to find you.

Sometimes it whispers.
Sometimes it laughs.
Sometimes it shows up wearing terrible timing and impeccable truth.

Either way, it's rising.

PART I

Reclaiming Joy

CHAPTER ONE

Joy All Over — The Joy of Travel

"Today, while the blossoms still cling to the vine,
I'll taste your strawberries,
I'll drink your sweet wine.
A million tomorrows will all pass away,
ere I forget all the joys that are mine today."
~ The New Christy Minstrels

Travel has always been one of the quickest ways for me to remember that my way of being in the world is not the only way—and often not the most interesting one. It shifts my assumptions. It humbles me. Sometimes it scares me. Sometimes it seduces me. Almost always, it teaches me something about joy that I didn't know I needed to learn.

This chapter isn't about bucket lists, luxury, or bragging rights. It's about what happens when you step outside your familiar patterns and let the world meet you where you actually are—messy, curious, hopeful, afraid, enchanted.

MEXICO CITY

Early in my marriage to my current and final husband, he was working on a movie being shot in Mexico. Another crew member's wife and I flew to Mexico City to meet them on their days off. We had never met before. We found each other at the airport, climbed into a taxi together, and pressed our faces to the windows, trying to take everything in at once. The colors. The chaos. The driving. Sometimes we couldn't open our eyes wide enough to see it all. Sometimes we had to close them entirely.

We spent the weekend in Mexico City with our men, eating incredible food, wandering, laughing, and soaking it all in. Then we traveled a couple of hours away to a much smaller town where the filming was actually happening. It felt remote, dusty, and intimate—nothing like the city we'd just left behind.

On the morning we were supposed to leave, our husbands had arranged for us to be driven back to the airport in the film truck—something the crew did regularly to transport film canisters back to the States. It was a protective plan, born out of real concern. At the time, there were widespread reports of Americans being kidnapped for ransom, often involving a specific fleet of small green taxis. It was a big deal for the two of us to be traveling "alone" at all.

Our husbands had to be on set at 4 a.m. Our flight didn't depart until 10. We slept in a bit, packed, and went downstairs at 7 to meet the truck.

There was no truck.

Instead, we were met by a confused crew member who told us, very casually, that no film truck was coming.

Cue panic.

We called a taxi. What arrived was an old jalopy with no front passenger seat. Our luggage went where the seat should have been. It was immediately clear this car was not going to make it to Mexico City, let alone the airport, and certainly not in time. We asked—politely and urgently—to be taken to the bus station.

We made it onto a bus, paid a child collecting fares in the aisle, and I asked in my broken Spanish whether this bus went to the airport. "Sí, sí," he said cheerfully.

A couple of hours later, we arrived at a central bus station in Mexico City. Not the airport. Not even close. We had less than an hour before our flight.

At this point, the fear felt very real.

The taxi line was impossibly long. Then a man ran up to us, grabbed our luggage, and said, "You need airport now?" as he ran off. We ran after him because what choice did we have? He led us straight to those infamous little green taxis.

I was terrified.

I met the driver, who spoke no English. I asked him in my middle-school Spanish, "Buen Señor, ¿es seguro esto?" Good Sir, is this safe? I received the same answer I had been getting all morning: "Si. Si. Si." I looked him in the eye, extended my hand, and said, "No, señor. Con su promesa, ¿es seguro?" No, Sir. With your promise, is this safe?

He looked back at me and said, "Sí, Señora," then shook my hand.

He drove like a bat out of hell—which, it turns out, is how everyone drives in Mexico City—but the entire way he pointed out signs and landmarks, saying, "Mira, mira. Aeropuerto." Look, look. Airport.

He got us there. I handed him all the Mexican money I had. We ran through the terminal like we were escaping a burning building. They were closing the doors just as we boarded. The plane took off almost immediately. Only then did we exhale.

When our husbands got back to the hotel later that day and discovered there had been no truck, they were furious and terrified. It was a few hours before we connected and reassured them that we were safe. That care they had taken—those plans that fell apart—mattered more to me than the danger itself.

Looking back, what stays with me most isn't the danger but the strange mix of adventure and pride we felt. We had been scared, yes—but also resourceful. In the end, what got us there safely wasn't a plan, a system, or a truck. It was a human-to-human moment: a kind man who saw two frightened women, helped them reach their destination, and made sure they felt safe along the way.

ISTANBUL

Years later, after the adrenaline and improvisation of Mexico City, I committed myself to a future of luxury travel, full of champagne and safety. I wanted to see the world, but I didn't want to compromise on safety and security. I have since found that those two things are not only overrated but are really illusions.

Recently, we enjoyed a bucket-list cruise through the Mediterranean. We sailed into Istanbul on the Bosphorus. Istanbul sits on two continents—Europe and Asia—and somehow manages to hold ancient history and modern life side by side.

It was August. Hot doesn't begin to cover it. It felt like vacationing on the surface of the sun! The ocean breeze felt more like mercy than weather.

The city was an assault on the senses in the best possible way. The spice market was thick with color and scent—cardamom, cumin, saffron, dried fruit, roasting nuts. I delighted in haggling with vendors, feeling extremely proud of what I was sure were excellent bargains... until I later realized I had spent well over a thousand dollars on tea, candy, spices, and enough saffron to supply a small restaurant for decades. If anyone reading this needs a lead on Persian saffron, I'm your girl.

We were treated to a private baklava and Turkish coffee tasting—two things I had never thought much about before. There in Istanbul, as our hosts carefully curated these delicacies for us, I was overwhelmed with gratitude for the depth of the experience. These weren't just foods or beverages. They were cultural sensory explosions. And don't even get me started on Turkish delight. I came home with five pounds of it!

We visited the Hagia Sophia—once a church, then a mosque, and now a mosque and a major tourist attraction. Outside, a woman sold disposable headscarves to female tourists for a dollar. We bought them and covered our heads before entering. Before we went in, a female guide quietly took the women in our group aside and told us that if any of us were on our period, we were not to enter. She didn't say why. She didn't need to. The implication was clear: menstruating women are considered unclean.

On one hand, I was oddly flattered—it had been decades since that could possibly apply to me. On the other hand, mind your own business.

Inside, armed guards patrolled the space. Watching them suddenly descend on a blonde American woman in our group, whose head covering slipped just enough to reveal a bit of hair, was deeply unsettling. It was abrupt, intimidating, and frightening. It quickly became clear they weren't there to protect us. They were there to control us. When I say us, I mean the women.

What made this even more disorienting was the contrast outside those walls. Istanbul's nightlife was decadent, loud, sensual, and unapologetically alive. The same streets that demanded modesty by day pulsed with music, laughter, and desire by night. It wasn't hypocrisy so much as contradiction—layers of history, power, pleasure, fear, and control stacked on top of one another.

As an American woman, I felt pulled in opposite directions at once. Part of me wanted to stand tall, be seen, be heard, and be exactly who I am. Another part of me felt acutely aware that I was in a place where women's bodies were not neutral—they were regulated, judged, and watched. I wanted to be invisible.

Every morning before heading out, I'd sing myself a little reminder: "Head, shoulders, knees and toes, head, shoulders, knees and toes—better cover all of those." It became a kind of private joke, a way to brace myself for the day.

Then it struck me that this wasn't just about travel. It wasn't just about religion, culture, or politics. It was about what it feels like to move through the world when your body is treated as a problem to be managed. It was about having to calculate what you wear, where you go, how you speak, and how visible you allow yourself to be—every single day.

For a brief time, I could step out of that experience and return to the relative safety of being a middle-aged American woman with a passport and a plane ticket home. But for many people—women, people of color, LGBTQ folks, and the disabled—there is no leaving it behind. This is what they deal with every day of their lives. That vigilance, that awareness, that quiet calculation is simply the cost of existing.

Istanbul didn't make me feel afraid. It made me feel awake. It reminded me that joy, freedom, and safety are not evenly distributed, and that noticing this is not a burden. It's a responsibility.

TROY

From Istanbul, we traveled to Troy. It was still Turkey, but I felt more at ease on the shore and in the countryside. I felt less like easy prey for overzealous salesmanship and less judged for my femaleness.

Standing there was surreal. This was not just another archaeological site or tourist stop—it was *the* Troy. The place I had read about in school, the place of legend and myth, so deeply layered with history that it felt almost unreal underfoot.

There are at least six distinct layers of Troy, stacked one atop another. City built. City conquered. City burned. City abandoned. City rebuilt. Again and again. Walking through the excavation felt like walking through time itself, each layer a reminder that human ambition, desire, and conflict have repeated themselves for a very long time. Apparently, we are nothing if not consistent.

What struck me most was how small Troy actually was. Just a modest area near the coast. And yet, its location was so strategically powerful that for centuries, generations of civilizations rose and fell there. So much bloodshed, so much mythology, so much storytelling—all centered on a place you could stroll across in an hour. It really messes with your sense of scale... and importance.

And then there was Helen.

After all, this was the place that launched a thousand ships.

The face that launched a thousand ships.

Beauty so powerful it became legend.

Desire so potent it justified war.

(Which feels like a lot to put on one woman, honestly.)

Standing there, I couldn't help but feel the weight of the juxtaposition. This place once celebrated beauty and longing so intensely that it reshaped history. Just days earlier in Istanbul, I had been in spaces where women were required to cover themselves and were monitored, corrected, and controlled. Where beauty was something to be hidden, managed, and feared.

The contrast was stark.

Helen's beauty was mythologized, weaponized, blamed, and immortalized. Thousands died because of it. Centuries later, women's bodies are still treated as dangerous—something to regulate rather than revere. Different century, same discomfort.

And yet.

Despite all the wars, the destruction, the layers of conquest, what stayed with me most was not despair. It was resilience. The fact that people kept rebuilding. That life returned. That joy, somehow, persisted. Even after humanity did what it does best, fighting itself.

Troy reminded me that joy doesn't disappear just because humans make a mess of things. It waits. It resurfaces. It survives beneath the rubble.

Standing there, I felt small—and oddly comforted. We have been struggling with the same questions for thousands of years. And still, we find reasons to love, desire, create, and rebuild.

Joy has always been part of the story, even here.

TUNISIA (CARTHAGE)

From Troy, we sailed south and crossed into Africa.

I was more excited than I expected to be. I realized I had never set foot on the African continent before, and something about that mattered to me in a way I didn't fully understand until we arrived. Tunisia sits on the ancient city of Carthage, and everywhere you look, there are layers of history—Phoenicians, Romans, empires stacked like sediment.

Aqueducts still stretch across the landscape. Ruins appear without fanfare, just there, woven into daily life. You don't have to imagine history here.

You trip over it.

What fascinated me most, though, wasn't the ruins.

It was the people I didn't see.

As we walked through Carthage, I realized that the only Black people I saw were Americans from our ship. That stopped me short. Africa, in my mind, had always been imagined as Black. And here I stood on African soil, surrounded by history, culture, and beauty—yet confronted with the complicated realities of colonization, migration, power, and erasure.

It was unsettling and instructive.

Travel has a way of gently dismantling the stories you didn't even know you were telling yourself. I realize now that I was looking for Black people the way one expects to see Mickey and Minnie at Disneyland. I needed to experience it as it actually was in order to learn from it. We visited an American military cemetery there, a reminder of those who fought and died on the continent during WWII. I was pleased and impressed to find a tribute to the Tuskegee Airmen. It felt like a beautiful tribute to a people who were once kidnapped and enslaved and are now honored as heroes in the land of their ancestors.

Tunisia didn't explain itself to me. It didn't offer a neat narrative or a tidy moral. It simply existed—layered, complicated, shaped by forces far older and far larger than me.

I left with more questions than answers. I've come to believe that is one of the signs that travel is doing its job.

GREECE

Greece felt like home.

Not in a nostalgic way, nor in a "past life" way—just in a bodily, unmistakable sense of belonging. From the moment we arrived, I felt welcomed rather than observed, included rather than evaluated. I loved the water, the clothes, the food, and the people. I didn't feel separate from the centuries of culture and history—I felt folded into it, as if someone had quietly made room for me at the table.

ATHENS

Athens is a modern, living city layered directly on top of itself. Coffee shops, traffic, and everyday errands unfold alongside ruins that predate most of what we call civilization. You can turn a corner and suddenly stand next to something you studied in high school—except it's real, enormous, and inconveniently uphill.

As we made our way through the Acropolis and the Parthenon, what struck me was how casually the Greeks carry their history. These aren't relics kept at a distance. They're companions, old friends who just happen to be thousands of years old.

After years of watching *My Big Fat Greek Wedding* and laughing at the father who insists that every word originates in Greek, I can now confirm that every Greek I met did exactly the same thing.

And the thing is—they're not wrong.

There's something humbling about realizing you're speaking with people whose ancestors invented the very words that shape how we think—and who are still happy to correct you.

From the vast sweep of empires and ideas in Athens, Greece, gently brought us back to the human scale.

PATMOS

In Patmos, we were welcomed into a family-run restaurant where three generations worked together. The food was simple, generous, and deeply satisfying—the kind of meal that felt like it had been cooked many times before and perfected through love rather than ambition. No foam. No deconstruction. Just food that welcomed, nourished, and satisfied.

After we ate, the family performed for us. They sang and danced on a small stage, dressed in traditional clothing of wool vests, hats, and long-sleeved embroidered finery... in 100-degree weather! I cannot recall or even conceive of a time when I was that hospitable under such conditions. They offered music and movement that clearly carried history and pride. The performance felt like an offering, shared with dignity and confidence.

I didn't feel like a tourist being entertained. I felt like a guest being welcomed into something real and shared joyously.

SANTORINI

Santorini was breathtaking in that almost unfair way. White houses stacked along cliffs, blue roofs rising from an even bluer sea, light everywhere. It was so iconic...

So iconic that six cruise ships were anchored off the coast the same day we were there! We decided to avoid the crowds as best we could and spent an idyllic day at the beach. The crush was trying to get on and off the island. I could almost feel that small, beautiful place groan under the weight of ten thousand extra tourists.

But the people there weren't groaning. They were hospitable, welcoming, and genuinely interested in their guests. Every local we met wanted to hear about our lives and where we were from. We shared stories, snacks, and laughs. Every shop and restaurant felt like visiting a friend's house.

I didn't feel like I needed to do anything there. I felt lucky to be allowed to be present.

Sometimes joy is exactly that—just being present.

RHODES

Rhodes is beautiful, historic, and on the water, like the rest of Greece. But Rhodes is where I felt a deep, personal human connection.

On our first visit, I was exploring the old town and pawing through racks of clothes on the street. I struck up a conversation with the shopkeeper, who greeted me and asked how I was. When I asked how she was, she answered honestly—she'd just had an interaction with a rude, insulting customer and was still shaken by it. The customer, it turned out, was American. From our ship. Of course.

I apologized—not performatively but sincerely. I apologized for my countrymen and for all those whose entitlement causes them to ignore human kindness.

My husband joined me, and we went into her shop. We tried on almost everything. We ended up buying half of what we tried on, and she gave us the rest as gifts. We spent hours in her store, sitting, talking, meeting her family, and sharing a cool drink.

When we left, we carried bags full of purchases, gifts, and goodwill.

A week later, we returned to Rhodes and decided to stop by her shop just to say hello. It turns out that just saying hello is impossible in Rhodes. Of course, she remembered us. Out came the coffee. More conversation. More warmth. I casually mentioned how much I loved the lemon gelato I had tasted in Greece. Moments later, the gelato shop owner up the street appeared with lemon gelato for all of us.

We never learned her name.

But the things we brought home from that shop still carry the memory of being welcomed—not as tourists but as friends.

COPENHAGEN

Copenhagen was my first trip to Europe. It was also the trip where everything went sideways.

We went because of my husband's work. I tagged along, thrilled to finally see Europe for the first time, excited to wander through museums and cafés and soak up a city I had only ever imagined. Instead, I learned what it feels like to be held, almost cradled, by a place, a system, and strangers when your life suddenly falls apart.

My husband was working with the San Francisco Ballet, which was performing in Copenhagen for the Queen of Denmark. There were rehearsals, anticipation, and that electric opening-night energy. I noticed he wasn't feeling well, but he powered through—because of course he did. He performed on opening night, and I stood in the audience, applauding wildly and bursting with pride.

That night, he was transported to the hospital by ambulance.

He stayed there for three weeks.

We were supposed to be in Copenhagen for eight days, but we stayed nearly thirty. During that time, he had seven surgeries.

On the day the ballet company was scheduled to leave, I stood in the hotel lobby, watching dancers and crew load their luggage into vans heading to the airport. I remember feeling like the last kid left at daycare—standing there, alone in a foreign country, wondering how, or if, my husband was going to survive this, and how I was going to get through it.

I didn't know how to get around the city. I didn't know the language... which was impossible. Thank God for British imperialism—almost everybody spoke English. At first, I relied on taxis—about fifty dollars a day, back and forth between the hotel and the hospital.

Then I remembered something improbable and wonderful: a close friend from high school had been a Danish exchange student. That was over four decades ago. We had lost touch, but thankfully, Facebook exists.

I found her.

She answered immediately. "I'm here," she said. She took a day off work, picked me up, and announced, "Today you're going to the Danish transportation school."

She got me a transit pass. She taught me how to use the buses, trains, and the subway. She showed me how to get to the hospital and back, and how to navigate the city with confidence rather than fear. She didn't drive me around or coddle me. She gave me my independence.

She also showed me Copenhagen. One of the places she took me was Elsinore—Hamlet's castle. Yes, that Hamlet. Standing there, looking out the window from the room said to be his, I could see Sweden across the water, and suddenly things I had only read about in high school became tangible.

Copenhagen loves Hans Christian Andersen the way cities usually reserve for pop stars. He is everywhere. Statues, stories, pride. The Little Mermaid sits quietly in the harbor, still doing her thing, unfazed by tourists or time.

One of the strange realities of the trip's extension was that I still had a company to run. I had expected to go home.

Every day followed the same rhythm. I spent the entire day at the hospital, then returned to the hotel in the evening. Because of the time difference, that's when my workday began. I was on calls, answering emails, and running my business late into the night. It was exhausting.

Actually, the only place I slept was at the hospital. I would crawl into the narrow bed beside my husband and rest.

The hospital staff were unfailingly kind. When they brought his meals, they also brought one for me, as if it were the most obvious thing in the world that I belonged there, too.

My husband was understandably depressed, in pain, and frightened about his health. He had two roommates. Before he could sink too deeply into despair, one of them said, "Well, at least you have a wife who visits you. No one's come to visit us."

It was a quiet, sobering perspective builder.

Every day, as I traveled across the city, I saw the same sights I see at home: parents hustling kids to school, people walking dogs and picking up poop, commuters heading to work, and shopkeepers opening their doors. We are far more alike than we pretend to be.

One morning, I stopped at the same bodega I visited daily to buy Coca-Cola—my husband was craving it desperately. I explained to the owner why I was there and why I needed Coke every day. He laughed and said, “Are you trying to kill him?” Then he froze, caught himself, and asked, “Oh! I’m so sorry. Is he dying?”

That question held everything: humor, humanity, and care.

When my husband was finally released from the hospital, it was just days before we were scheduled to fly home. I was trying to care for him in our tiny hotel room, barely big enough for one. I kept going out frequently to find food for him that could be transported and eaten in that cramped space, while dealing with the new reality of his compromised body. He wasn’t doing well. I was terrified. I called the hospital, and the person who answered knew us—knew his name, my name, our story.

“If he’s not doing well,” they said, “just bring him back. We’ll check him out. If we need to readmit him, we will. Do you need an ambulance, or can you take a taxi?”

I remember thinking, I don’t think you people are speaking English correctly.

This would never happen in the United States.

They never once asked me for money. After days in the hospital, they handed me half a sheet of paper to fill out—his name, date of birth, my name, and my local address.

That was it.

Copenhagen saved my husband’s life. They did it cheerfully, thoroughly, and without drama. It would turn out to be the beginning of a years-long medical journey—two to three years marked by numerous surgeries, recovery, and uncertainty—but I will always believe that if we hadn’t been there, if we had tried to fly home instead of going to the hospital that night, he wouldn't have survived the flight.

Everywhere I went, I kept thinking, "Oh! My husband would love it here!"

He never really got to see Copenhagen. I saw it for him. I took pictures every day and brought them back to the hospital, showing them to him when he was lucid enough to look. The streets, the harbor, the quiet order of the city, and the ordinary beauty of people going about their lives.

In that way, he was there too—held by the same place that held us both.

TAHITI

Tahiti changed my perspective—literally.

This was my first trip to the Southern Hemisphere, and I didn't realize how disorienting it would be until one night, when I looked up at the sky and didn't recognize it. The stars were different and the constellations unfamiliar. It was the same universe, but viewed through an entirely different window.

Ninety percent of the world's human population lives in the Northern Hemisphere. We build our systems, maps, and assumptions from that vantage point. Down South, the world feels less human-centric and more attuned to nature. The land doesn't organize itself around us. We are clearly visitors.

That realization alone was worth the trip.

We were traveling through French Polynesia—Bora Bora, Moorea, Nuka Hiva—moving between islands that felt like one paradise after another. Water, mountains, sky, reef. Life operating perfectly without asking for our input.

One afternoon, after snorkeling with sharks and rays while docked in the lagoon, we were resting in our cabin when we turned on the television. *Mutiny on the Bounty*—the Mel Gibson version—was playing.

I looked out from our balcony and realized we were anchored exactly where it had been filmed, the site of the historical mutiny.

And suddenly, I understood it completely.

Who would willingly leave this place to board a cramped wooden ship, wear wool uniforms, be lashed as punishment, and have their rum rationed? How arrogant Westerners are! They believe ours is the only civilization and that the exploitation of people and resources is the only way to live on the planet. Paradise has a way of making authority both feel extremely theoretical and totally out of place.

Like many enchanted visitors before us, we spent part of the trip half-joking, half-scheming about how we could stay forever. We even came up with what we were sure was a brilliant business idea that would let us do so—elegant, sustainable, and clearly destined for success.

The next day, we went jet skiing.

Timmy was our guide. Every other couple shared a jet ski, with the women riding behind their men, clinging on for dear life. I decided I wanted to be on my own machine. Even though I had never jet-skied before, my husband knew better than to argue with me. I was more scared and tentative than I expected, and at first, Timmy worried I wouldn't be able to keep up with the group. I won't pretend I was graceful or even competent, but I did it. It was thrilling, and I was proud of myself for doing it.

At one point, we shared our brilliant business plan with Timmy and invited him to partner with us.

He listened politely. Then he spread his arms wide, gesturing towards the lagoon, the mountains, the water, and the sky, and said:

"What do I need money for? I live here."

That sentence stopped us cold.

From his point of view, he already had what mattered. Place. Community. Beauty. Enough. The idea that paradise needed improving was entirely ours.

Timmy wasn't naïve. He wasn't unambitious. He was simply content.

And there we were—two well-meaning Americans, trying to solve a problem that didn't exist.

Tahiti didn't lecture us. It didn't need to. It simply showed us another way to be in the world—one where humans are not the center of the story but part of it.

When you've spent your whole life looking out one window, realizing there are others can be quietly revolutionary.

I want to be clear about one thing. I didn't write this chapter to catalog luxury trips or brag about where I've been. That's what my social media feed is for. Luxury isn't required for joy, and travel doesn't have to involve planes, cruises, or passports—or tiny bottles of shampoo you can never quite open in the shower.

What travel does—at any scale—is remind us that joy is not owned by any one culture, country, or economic class. It exists wherever people do. Sometimes it shows up in a bustling city, sometimes in a quiet village, sometimes in a hospital room, sometimes in a sentence that stops you in your tracks.

Travel has taught me that joy is universal, connection is human, and perspective is always available if we're willing to look out a different window—even if that window is only a few miles or a few conversations away from home.

CHAPTER TWO

Joy of Sex

"Sex, like every other aspect of joy,
is our birthright."
~ Carolyn Pistone

Tahiti didn't just feel beautiful.

It felt sexy.

Historically, sexuality in Tahitian culture wasn't hidden or policed. It was expressive, playful, and reverent—a form of praise, a way to honor life and the gods themselves. Bodies weren't problems to be managed. They were instruments of joy.

You could still feel traces of that worldview everywhere. In the drumming. In the dancing. In the way music and movement felt less like performance and more like participation in something ancient and alive.

One afternoon on Moorea, during a break on an island tour, I felt it in my body before I had a thought about it. I charged into the shallow lagoon—knee-deep, warm, clear water—and found myself dancing. No music. No audience. Just joy rising and asking to be expressed.

(There may or may not be video evidence of this, courtesy of my adoring husband.)

Another evening at a beach barbecue, local musicians played and sang while we ate. I wasn't dragged into the spotlight. I wasn't turned into a novelty. I was **invited to join**—with a look that said, *Share our joy, be part of it. You are welcome here*.

Later in the trip, those same performers came aboard our cruise ship to perform in the ship's theater. Suddenly, the energy shifted.

The performance was the same.

The audience was not.

What had felt celebratory and sexy on the island became something else entirely under the gaze of a largely American crowd. Some watched with appreciation and respect. A few—mostly older white men—leered openly, as if this were not a joyous shared cultural experience but rather a strip club they frequented.

It made me deeply uncomfortable... and embarrassed on behalf of my culture.

That contrast stayed with me. It still does.

Sex, when it's healthy and whole, is joyful, ridiculous, embodied, and alive. When it's stripped of context and reduced to a spectacle, it loses its humanity. Tahiti showed me the difference.

THE PUP TENT (OR ENTHUSIASM IS NOT A PLAN)

Long before Tahiti, long before menopause, long before I had any idea what I was doing, there was a boy I loved in high school and a plan that seemed excellent at the time.

We decided to sneak out at night for a romantic adventure. He came prepared, or so he thought.

We drove to a regional park, hiked to a secluded spot, and he proudly revealed his gear: a tent, a sleeping bag, and a flashlight.

What he had failed to consider was the scale.

We took turns holding the flashlight in our mouths while trying to set up the tent, which felt less like romance and more like a low-budget survival show. The tent was tiny, a Boy Scout pup tent. We rolled out the sleeping bag and crawled in. Once inside, we discovered that not only was the bag too small for both of us (it was a **mummy bag!**), but it also made it nearly impossible for me to open my legs at all, which was kind of the whole point of the adventure.

Adding to this, the woods at night are **cold, dark, and extremely noisy**. Every snap of a twig sounded like certain death. Every rustle felt like a bear... or a serial killer... or a serial-killer bear!

At some point—I don't remember who said it—one of us whispered, "We should go."

And that was it.

We grabbed everything, tripped over roots, abandoned all dignity, and sprinted back to the car like fugitives running from our own bad planning.

No magic. No romance. No sex.

Just laughter, relief, and the dawning realization that sex—or even the attempt at it—is often ridiculous. That's not a failure. It's part of the charm.

Looking back, I'm oddly grateful for that night. It taught me early on that joy doesn't require perfection, elegance, or even a properly sized sleeping bag.

Sometimes joy is just enthusiasm, a good story, and knowing when to run to the car.

A GRANDMOTHER'S WISDOM

My grandparents flew to California for my first wedding. My grandmother took me aside for a private talk. "There's something that's going to happen to you after you get married, and you're not going to like it." I was all ears! What was this woman, in her eighties, married for almost seventy years, and bringing the wisdom of generations, going to impart? "It's called a bladder infection, and you should drink cranberry juice." Well, she was nothing if not practical. And, of course, she was right.

THE ASSAULTS I COULD NOT NAME

For a long time, I didn't have the language for what had happened to me.

I wasn't dragged into an alley by a stranger. There were no dramatic scenes, no police reports, no courtroom reckonings. The men who assaulted me were men I knew. In some cases, they were men who were supposed to care for me or even love me.

It took me well into my fifties to even say the word *rape* to myself.

Part of the reason it took so long was that I had been taught—explicitly and implicitly—that my body came with conditions. That if I had had sex before, if I wasn't a virgin, if I wasn't married, if I wasn't a "good Christian girl," then harm didn't quite count as harm.

Consent, I learned later, was treated by some men as an all-access permission slip. Once granted, it was assumed to be permanent.

One of the men who raped me believed exactly that. Because I had slept with him before, he felt entitled to do it again—regardless of what I wanted. In his mind, no harm had been done. No rules had been broken.

Another assault occurred at a small Christian college. I was raped by a neighbor from my dorm in a study room in the library's basement. Afterward, he walked me home. He continued to live next door to me for the rest of the semester.

There were no consequences for him. No questions asked. I went to class. I passed him in the hallway. Life went on—except something in me had quietly broken... again.

I am certain none of the men who assaulted me believe they raped me. There was no reckoning for them. No cost or consequences. The burden of understanding, surviving, and integrating what had happened fell entirely on me.

Layered beneath all of this was childhood sexual abuse—the kind that teaches your nervous system, long before your mind understands what's happening, that your body is not fully your own.

So, I adapted. I survived. I learned to be affectionate, passionate, and warm—while remaining disconnected in ways I didn't yet recognize. I carried joy and trauma side by side, unaware they could be untangled.

For decades, I minimized. I reframed. I told myself stories that made everything seem smaller and safer than it actually was. I didn't want to see myself as a victim. I didn't want to believe that something so violating could have happened without leaving visible wreckage.

But harm doesn't require spectacle to be real.

What I know now is this: My body, my desire, and my sexuality belong to me. They always have. Others' failure to honor that truth does not diminish it.

And while the assaults impacted me, they did not get to define me.

This chapter exists not because trauma deserves the final word, but because naming it is part of reclaiming joy. And because silence never protected me anyway.

THE LOVER'S QUESTION

Sometime later—much later—a lover asked me a question that made me pause.

He knew about my history. About the abuse. About the assaults I had only recently learned to name. And one day, gently, without accusation or pity, he asked:

"How are you able to be so passionate... so affectionate... after everything you've been through?"

What a great question!

Here's the thing: My body didn't belong to the men who hurt me. It never did. If I allowed what they took to erase my desire, affection, and joy, then they would still be taking something from me that didn't belong to them. My body, my desire, and my sexuality belong to me. If I let fear or shame erase that, I would be surrendering something precious that was never theirs to take.

My passion isn't evidence that the trauma didn't happen.

It's proof that it didn't win.

I refuse to give up one of life's greatest gifts: hot, horny, ridiculous, joyful humping!

One of the other perks of surviving, I suppose, is that decades later you get to write a book about how great you are in bed.

This isn't denial.

It's defiance.

And it's joy!

MENOPAUSE (OR FREEDOM AT LAST)

There is a particular kind of wisdom that only comes from women who have known each other forever.

The girls I grew up with—middle school, first periods, first crushes, first heartbreaks—are still my people. We lost touch for decades, raised children, married, divorced, built lives, survived illnesses, and buried parents. When we finally found our way back to one another, we discovered something astonishing:

We had become exactly who we were always meant to be.

When we talk now, we talk about everything, especially sex.

One of the great revelations of menopause was realizing just how many "rules" about sex were never actually about pleasure. They were about control. About reproduction. About who gets to father children, who gets judged, who carries shame, and who gets forgiven.

And then menopause arrives and essentially says,

"Well, none of that applies anymore."

No risk of pregnancy. No biological compliance. No societal utility.

Just desire. Or not. Choice. Or not. Curiosity. Or not.

And suddenly, the whole thing becomes yours.

There is also something deeply liberating about reaching an age when you realize you are officially outside the demographic everyone is trying to manage. You can dress how you want. Want sex? Great. Don't want sex? Also, great. Want it enthusiastically on Tuesday and absolutely not on Wednesday? Congratulations—you are a free woman.

My friends and I talk openly now—about pleasure, bodies, aches and noises, and the fact that nothing works quite like it used to, but somehow that matters less. We laugh about hot flashes, lube, and the stunning realization that attraction does not, in fact, evaporate when estrogen does.

And here's the secret no one tells you:

Sex doesn't stop being joyful because your body changes.

It becomes more joyful *because* your body has lived.

Sex in later life does not become more graceful with experience.

There are glasses involved now. Actual eyeglasses that have a tendency to bang together at inopportune moments. There are limbs that fall asleep. Knees that make sounds they never used to make.

Sometimes we have to stop completely because someone gets a cramp.

In our old house, we had a gorgeous, marble, jacuzzi-style bathtub. It was stunning. Glamorous. Deeply suggestive. It looked like it belonged in a movie.

Watching either of us try to get in or out of it completely ruined the fantasy.

And yet—there we were. Still laughing. Still touching. Still delighted to be there at all.

And honestly? That's the triumph.

Not perfection. Not elegance. Not stamina measured against some imaginary standard.

The joy is that we're still doing it. Arthritis, skin tags, and flatulence be damned!

Still wanting it.

Still choosing affection, pleasure, and closeness.

At this point in life, sex isn't something you prove.

It's something you *celebrate*.

At some point along the way, I realized something important.

My body is not a cautionary tale.

My desire is not a problem to be managed.

My pleasure does not belong to my past, partners, trauma, or anyone else's expectations.

It belongs to me.

Sex, like joy, is not something we earn by being good, careful, or appropriate. It is something we get to *choose*. Again and again. With laughter. With tenderness. With curiosity.

And maybe that's the real victory.

Not flawless intimacy.

Not ageless performance.

But the freedom to stay in our bodies, laugh when things get ridiculous, and say yes to pleasure anyway.

Hot, horny, joyful, ridiculous humping included.

CHAPTER THREE

Joy During Suffering

"How wonderful it is that nobody need wait a single moment before starting to improve the world."
~ Anne Frank

"Why am I soft in the middle when the rest of my life is so hard?"
~ Paul Simon

Suffering has terrible timing.

It shows up uninvited, overstays its welcome, and rarely waits until you've cleared your calendar or finished your coffee.

For a long time, I thought joy was supposed to excuse itself during those moments.

But joy doesn't seem to know the rules.

It shows up anyway. In the middle of grief. In the middle of fear. Sometimes, while you're absolutely certain you are not handling things "well."

I've learned this: Joy during suffering isn't denial.

It's defiance.

It's the quiet insistence that when life is brutal, unfair, or terrifying, it doesn't get to take everything. It's the part of us that refuses to disappear, even when circumstances suggest it would be more polite to do so.

This chapter isn't about minimizing pain.

It's about what happens when joy shows up, regardless, and why I've come to trust it when it does.

MY GRANDFATHER

When I think about joy during suffering, I first think of my maternal grandfather.

All my grandparents were immigrants, but my grandfather's story begins in a way that could have been written by Charles Dickens.

He was an orphan in Poland. A little boy—six or seven years old—was brought to the United States by a couple of "aunts." He was sent to live with an "uncle" in Minnesota who owned a farm.

I put *uncle* and *aunts* in quotation marks because, looking back, I don't know if these people were relatives at all.

What I now suspect—through adult eyes and through the lens of everything I've learned about how vulnerable children are exploited—is that my grandfather may have been a trafficked child laborer. A small orphan boy shipped across an ocean and handed off to someone who needed free hands on a farm.

He lived in the barn. He slept in the barn. He did nothing but farm work.

He was treated like an animal.

He didn't talk about it much, but I know he was beaten. I know he was starved. I know he was treated cruelly. At some point, because he had whatever kind of fierce will it takes to survive a life like that, he ran away.

Somehow, he made his way to the streets of Milwaukee, Wisconsin. Selling newspapers. Scraping by. Whatever hard, hard-scrabble things a little boy does when no one is coming to rescue him.

Then he met my grandmother. They were both candy factory workers. They married and built a life that looked ordinary from the outside.

But what I remember most about my grandfather is not the brutality of how his life started.

It's the tenderness of who he became.

He was the sweetest, kindest, most loving, and most generous man I ever knew. In my childhood, there was no safer place than on his lap or in his arms.

He never had money. He was never powerful. He wasn't "important" in the way the world defines important. But he was filled with love. He was a happy man. And nothing made him happier than his family.

Both my grandparents were charitable. They volunteered during the war, including at the USO. When they retired (*in their eighties*), they volunteered to help what they called "the old people" at the old people's home. They'd help them on and off the bus, serve meals, and do whatever needed to be done.

I think about that now, and I'm like... you're eighty-something years old, and your volunteer work is helping the elderly.

And then there's this small detail that still makes me tear up.

Because of his humble beginnings, he never went to school. He only learned to read and write minimally. When I was a child, he would send birthday cards with a chicken-scratch scrawl: *Happy birthday. Stay healthy. Love you*. And inside there was cash. Usually, a couple of dollars—often matching whatever age I was at the time.

It wasn't until he died that we began receiving beautiful, perfectly written letters from my grandmother with actual checks enclosed. That's when we realized that for their whole marriage, she had just... allowed him to lead as the man. And now it turned out she was the educated one. The "brains."

About two years after my grandfather died, my grandmother was napping in her armchair. She woke up and said he had appeared to her, dressed in his finery, and had said, "It's time for you to come with me now, Sarah."

She died two days later.

Here's what I can't get over: By any normal logic, that little orphan boy had every reason to grow up hard, bitter, closed-off, and mean.

Instead, he became the gentlest man I ever knew.

So, when I'm tempted to think *I can't be joyous because life has been cruel,* I think of him.

Not because suffering is romantic. God, no.

But because joy—real joy—can survive what we think should destroy it.

And sometimes it survives **because** someone chooses to keep their heart soft anyway.

Joy did not erase his suffering, but it endured it.

MY FATHER

My father was born in 1927, a product of the Roaring Twenties, and his childhood offered him very little in the way of safety or tenderness.

His parents were in an arranged marriage and did not love each other. There was poverty. There was drinking. His father was a notorious alcoholic. His work was glazing windows—often while drinking. One day, on a sixth-story job, he failed to fasten his safety belt properly and fell.

The fact that he was likely drunk at the time probably saved his life.

He survived the fall, but he was paralyzed from the waist down and spent the rest of his life in a wheelchair.

Before the accident, my grandfather beat my grandmother horribly. After the accident, he blamed her, saying it was her fault because she had cursed him when he came home drunk. From that point on, bitterness and resentment became permanent residents in the house.

This was the home my father grew up in.

When he was fourteen, he ran away.

Fourteen!

He lied about his age, changed his name, and joined the Merchant Marines at the start of World War II. I've often wondered how bad a child's home life has to be for that child to decide that war—across an ocean—sounded preferable.

And yet, when I think of my father, what I remember most is not the damage.

It's the joy.

He was always the life of the party. A jazz musician in San Francisco in the 1960s. An accomplished cook. Later, after an early retirement from advertising, he became an actor and spent more than forty years onstage, clearly enjoying himself and delighted that anyone else would watch.

If I ever lost him in a crowded place—an airport, a grocery store, anywhere—I knew exactly how to find him.

I would just listen.

He was always singing.

I'm not saying he was the best dad, husband, or man, maybe not even a very good one, but his life is a testament to joy and resilience.

In his late nineties, my father found himself swept up in something extraordinary. As one of the last surviving World War II veterans, he became involved with the Gary Sinise Foundation and its efforts to honor veterans. On the eightieth anniversary of D-Day, he traveled to Normandy. My sister went with him because, at ninety-eight, he needed a caregiver.

We now like to joke that traveling with him was like traveling with Beyoncé.

Everywhere they went, there were parades. Ceremonies. Brass bands. Crowds. He was greeted, applauded, and thanked. Treated like royalty—because in that moment, he was. People lined up to shake his hand, look him in the eye, and say, "Because of you, I exist."

Before the trip, the Gary Sinise Foundation reached out to families and asked us to write letters to the veterans. During the war, mail calls were one of the things soldiers treasured most. They wanted to recreate that—to offer something personal and grounding amid all the ceremony.

I wrote a letter to my father:

Honored WWII Veteran
80th D Day Anniversary
May 26, 2024

Dear Dad,

Thank you for reading this. Thank you for your bravery and sacrifice and for surviving. Thank you for keeping your head, keeping your optimism, and keeping your humor, and passing it on. I know that you were just a boy when you went off to fight in the last great war and you may not have known what a great sacrifice it would be, or what courage it would require. That is the gift of youth. Please know that the world is a better place because of you and that I often think of your struggle and draw inspiration from it when I am facing challenges in my own life.

Any adventure, thrill, or joy you have received in the last 80 years is a direct result of your efforts during that brief and terrifying time. Any adventure, thrill, or joy that I experience or cause is also a direct result of those efforts. Thank you most of all, for finding your way to San Francisco and allowing me to be born and live most of my life in this beautiful place, surrounded by amazing people on this beautiful planet.

I know that the experiences of this war changed you forever and that you may not ever fully process the trauma. This is the gift of age and wisdom. I am grateful to the people that have chosen to remember and honor you on this important day. During these once again terrifying times, it is important to know that humans have faced such dark times before and in the end humanity prevails.

Please accept and enjoy the accolades you are receiving now.
It is important for the world to witness.
I love you, Dad. I'm so proud of you.
With Love and Gratitude,
Carolyn

What moves me most about this isn't just the honor or the spectacle.

It's the arc.

A boy raised in violence.

A teenager who fled.

A man who chose music, laughter, cooking, and the stage.

And decades later, an old man on a beach in France, receiving mail and being celebrated.

Joy didn't erase what he had lived through.

But it outlived it.

GRIEF HAS A SEAT AT THE TABLE

After my mother died, I was floundering. I was functioning, technically. Life was moving forward, but grief kept showing up unannounced. It was confusing, given the complicated relationship my mother and I had—one that defines most mother-daughter relationships. Ultimately, every love relationship interrupted by death feels unfinished. I somehow felt cheated by death, as if I were entitled to more than I got.

It was my mother's best friend who finally gave me words that made sense of what I was experiencing.

She said, *"You need to set a place for grief at your table."*

At first, I didn't fully understand what she meant. I think part of me hoped she was offering a strategy to make grief leave. But that wasn't the point at all.

What she was saying was that grief isn't something you can banish. It's something you live with.

Grief, it turns out, is a long-term guest. You don't have to let it sit at the head of the table or dominate every conversation. But pretending it isn't there only makes it knock harder.

So, I tried her way.

I imagined pulling out a chair for grief and letting it sit down. Not to run the meal. Not to ruin everything. Just to be acknowledged.

Something surprising happened when I did that.

Grief softened.

It didn't disappear, but it stopped ambushing me so violently. When I stopped fighting it, it stopped fighting back. And once grief had its place, something else began to return to the table too.

Joy.

Not the reckless, oblivious joy of before. A quieter joy. A sturdier one. The kind that knows loss exists and shows up anyway. The kind that can sit across from grief without being threatened by it.

I learned that grief and joy are not opposites. They are companions who can coexist, and often do.

ANNE FRANK: JOY THAT OUTLIVES TERROR

Anne Frank was a young teenager hiding in an attic nearly a hundred years ago.

She was not writing from a place of safety, comfort, or certainty. She was living under constant threat. She was cramped, frightened, bored, angry, hopeful, and acutely aware that her life could end at any moment.

And yet.

Her words are still here.

Not just her fear. Not just the horror of what she endured. Her joy. Her curiosity. Her belief in people. Her ability to notice beauty, irritation, humor, and longing—all of it—under conditions meant to crush the human spirit.

What moves me most about Anne Frank is not that she suffered. Millions suffered. It's that her joy survived.

She was not naïve. She was not shielded from reality. She knew cruelty and injustice intimately. And still, she wrote:

> *"In spite of everything, I still believe that people are really good at heart."*

That sentence didn't come from someone who hadn't seen darkness. It came from someone who had stared directly into it and refused to let it take everything.

Anne Frank didn't live long enough to see the world remember her. The fact that her words still ripple outward—still comforting, challenging, and illuminating—feels like a quiet rebellion against the forces that tried to erase her.

Her joy did not save her life.

But it did outlive terror.

And it continues to affect people—generations later—who never knew her.

That matters.

It reminds me that joy is not a reward for surviving. It's not something that arrives only after danger passes. Sometimes joy is the act of noticing, recording, loving, and believing—*while* the danger is still very much present.

That is why joy, even in times of suffering, is never frivolous.

It's defiant.

SAN QUENTIN: JOY INSIDE THE WALLS

I was invited to San Quentin to attend a theater program for inmates.

I had driven past San Quentin my entire life—past those walls, those towers, that looming sense of finality—without ever imagining what it would be like inside. I always assumed it would be easy to get in and nearly impossible to get out.

It turns out, getting in is the hard part.

There were forms, numerous checkpoints, and instructions on what not to wear, what not to bring, and what not to do. By the time we were finally allowed through the gates, I felt like I had already committed some kind of minor felony just for existing incorrectly.

The event was held in the largest chapel on the prison grounds. Inmates performed a Shakespeare play for other inmates, followed by original scenes they had written—vignettes drawn from their own lives, and inspired by the themes of the play.

As we entered the chapel and found an available pew, my husband—being the gentleman he is—stepped aside to let me go first.

That is how I, a small white woman, ended up sitting directly next to a very large Black man serving a very long sentence.

Neither of us clocked it at first. It was only after a particularly confusing performance ended that he leaned over and whispered to me, completely sincere.

"Did you get that?"

I smiled and said, "Not at all. I thought it was some kind of inside joke, and I was going to ask *you*."

We both laughed.

And just like that, the walls fell away a little.

After the performances, there was a Q&A with the actors. Each man introduced himself by name—and then by the length of his sentence.

One said his sentence ended "when doves cry."

Meaning: Never.

At the time, my son was in serious trouble with the law. The last time I had spoken to him was through glass. I stood up to ask a question, and before I knew it, I was telling the truth.

I said I had driven past San Quentin my entire life, but this was the first time they had ever invited me inside. I said I had a son and that during his worst years, I had told him that if he ever ended up here, I would not visit him.

And then I said out loud in that room:

"I'm sorry. I see now that there is hope here. And worth. None of you are my beautiful baby boy—but you are all somebody's."

When the program ended, several men came up to thank me for saying that. One told me his mother had said the same thing I had said to my son, and that he hadn't heard from her in twenty years.

What stayed with me most was this: Every single man who approached me asked the same question.

"How is your son?"

Not one of them asked about their own case, their own future, or what I thought of the performance.

They asked about my child.

The compassion within those walls surprised me, to say the least.

I walked into San Quentin expecting darkness. I found creativity. Humor. Insight. Accountability. Tenderness. Humanity.

Joy didn't belong there—at least not according to the story we tell ourselves about prisons and punishment.

And yet, there it was.

PERMISSION TO HEAL

During one of the hardest seasons of my life, I sometimes told my family I was running errands when I was really driving around so I could cry in private.

This was not a dramatic choice. It was a practical one. I needed somewhere to put the anguish, the fear, the exhaustion—and my car became the only place where I didn't have to hold it together for anyone else.

I would drive with no destination. Sometimes for hours. I'd pull over somewhere quiet and let myself fall apart. No witnesses. No fixing. Just breathing, crying, and waiting for the wave to pass.

What surprised me was that even in those drives—especially in those drives—joy kept showing up.

Not big joy. Not Instagram joy. Just little interruptions.

I live in a beautiful place. Most people do, if they look. I'd find myself driving through vineyards or along the Pacific cliffs, or through fog that hung low and silver over the land. One afternoon, driving home from one of my crying errands, I passed a miniature horse ranch.

The horses were miniature. The ranch was not.

The fog was just low enough that you couldn't see the ground. As the horses ran and played, their small bodies popped out of the mist like something out of a dream—or a children's book—or heaven, if that's your thing.

I remember thinking through my tears,

But look where I get to live.

That thought didn't erase the pain. It didn't fix anything. It didn't mean I was suddenly okay.

It just meant that anguish wasn't the only thing in the car with me anymore.

One evening, in the middle of everything—family crisis, illness, financial fear, the kind of season when you are just trying to survive—I was standing in my kitchen making dinner when I caught myself singing.

"Oh, what a beautiful morning..."

I stopped myself immediately.

What kind of monster sings show tunes while everything is falling apart?

And then I realized something important: This wasn't denial. This was healing beginning to knock.

Joy wasn't barging in. It wasn't demanding attention. It was just quietly reminding me that it still existed—and that I was allowed to let it back in.

Looking back, I can see that my willingness to feel joy again gave my family permission to do the same, though not all at once.

Joy didn't mean the suffering was over, but it helped remind all of us that it definitely wasn't permanent. And it helped us heal.

JOY IS NOT DENIAL

Some people think finding joy in the middle of suffering means you're ignoring reality.

I don't.

I think it means you're refusing to let suffering have exclusive rights to your life.

Joy is not pretending that things are fine when they're not.

Joy is not toxic positivity, spiritual bypassing, or slapping a smiley face on despair and calling it growth.

Joy is permission.

Permission to laugh without first checking whether it's appropriate.

Permission to notice beauty without feeling guilty about it.

Permission to sing show tunes while the house is metaphorically on fire.

Grief doesn't go away. My mother's friend was right—it needs a seat at the table. But joy doesn't have to wait for grief to leave the room.

Joy doesn't erase loss. It reminds us we survived it.

Sometimes joy shows up in ridiculous ways—miniature horses in the fog, a song sneaking out of your mouth, a moment of connection you didn't expect. Not because things are easy, but because your nervous system finally gets a chance to exhale.

If suffering teaches us anything, it's this: Life is fragile. Unpredictable. Heartbreakingly temporary.

Which makes joy not irresponsible but essential.

I wish I could tell you I learned all of this through quiet contemplation and spiritual maturity.

I did not.

I learned it because grief is exhausting, and at some point your nervous system says, *Okay, we're going to need a snack and a laugh, or we are not surviving this.*

Because sometimes the most radical act in the middle of suffering isn't courage, wisdom, or grace.

Sometimes it's simply about letting yourself enjoy the moment—without asking for permission or apologizing afterward.

Grief may need a permanent place at the table, but joy still gets to pass the bread, refill the wine, and occasionally tell a terrible joke.

"It takes grace to remain kind in cruel situations. Kindness isn't weak. It's the quiet roar of strength when the world shows its teeth, snarling and ready to bite. It's easy to grow claws in return. But grace, grace stands there battered and bruised but still chooses to extend an open hand. That's the real fight, to stay soft, to stay human when life tries to harden you into something less. Grace is the armor of the brave, worn not for glory but for the soul."

~ Peaky Blinders

PART II

Joy as Practice

CHAPTER FOUR

Joy and Integrity at Work

"It is difficult to get a man to understand something when his salary depends upon his not understanding it."
~ Upton Sinclair

I've spent most of my life working. Some of it was glamorous, some terrifying, some deeply boring, and some life-saving in ways I didn't recognize until much later. I've had jobs that impressed people at dinner parties and others that required steel-toed boots, sunscreen, and a very flexible definition of dignity.

What I've learned is this: Joy at work has almost nothing to do with status, salary, or job titles. It has everything to do with meaning, integrity, and whether you can look yourself in the mirror at the end of the day without needing a drink first. (Though sometimes you still want one. Let's be honest.)

WHEN WORK TURNS INTO A JOHN GRISHAM NOVEL (THAT NO ONE ASKED FOR)

I wasn't looking for corruption.

I want to be very clear about this, because I think people imagine these moments as cinematic—dark rooms, whispered threats, trench coats, maybe a dramatic envelope slid across a table. This was not that. This was meetings. Calendars. Emails. Contracts. Perfectly reasonable people using perfectly reasonable language to ask me to do something perfectly unreasonable.

Imagine being a purpose-driven business owner. A B Corp leader. Someone who genuinely believes that **how** you make money matters. Now imagine discovering that your biggest client—roughly ninety percent of your revenue, no pressure—was a major government contractor taking kickbacks from a publicly traded company.

And now imagine realizing you are right in the middle of it.

That's when I realized I had wandered into a John Grisham novel.

The first response was intimidation. Polite at first, then less so. The message was essentially: **This would all be much easier if you'd just stop noticing things.** They wanted me quiet. Out of the way. Invisible.

It would have been easy to comply. When I say "easy," I mean financially easy—not morally easy. Saying yes would have cost me more than money. It would have cost me my business license, my reputation, my integrity, and any ability to look myself in the mirror without resorting to selective amnesia.

So, I said no.

This surprised them.

Plan B was to offer me a "taste." Just enough to make it go away, and smooth things over. Just enough to compromise myself while maintaining plausible deniability. I believe the phrase "everyone does this" may have been uttered.

I said no again.

At this point, confusion set in. Genuine confusion. It had clearly not occurred to them that I might be serious about my values. Or that I might be stubborn. Or that I might be both.

I offered a compromise—not one that made me complicit, but one that let me extricate myself cleanly. It was a way to distance my company from the situation and free myself from the special hell of being a whistleblower. When they agreed, I learned something important:

They needed me more than I needed them.

I wish I could tell you that was the end of it and that everyone shook hands and went home wiser.

Instead, I spent the next year being maligned, threatened, and bullied. I lived with the low-grade terror of being a small-business owner caught between two billion-dollar companies and a government agency. I spent more time than I care to admit wondering whether my phone was tapped, my email was compromised, or if I was being wildly dramatic.

(It turns out you can be both vigilant **and** wildly dramatic at the same time.)

Maybe I was naïve. Maybe this is how business is done.

But it's wrong.

I couldn't do business that way.

Here's the thing about integrity: It is deeply inconvenient. It does not care about quarterly earnings, market pressures, or whether this is a "really bad time" to have principles. It shows up uninvited, demands consistency, and refuses to leave.

But once you choose it, something unexpected happens. You sleep better. You stand straighter. Even when you're scared—I was—you know exactly who you are.

If it had been easy to get around me or get rid of me, they would have. The fact that they couldn't told me everything I needed to know.

This experience didn't make me richer. It didn't make my life easier. It definitely didn't make me popular.

But it taught me something very important about myself. I have to stand by my values and integrity, no matter the stakes.

And it turns out that is a surprisingly joyful place to stand.

That kind of work tests your values. The next kind showed me why those values mattered.

THE LABOR CREW

You know how I like to say that if you lose enough jobs, you end up with a really great résumé?

Mine is... impressive.

During one particularly humbling three-year stretch of unemployment, the only job I could get was as a labor crew leader for at-risk youth in my county. I applied for it because I desperately needed the income and because it had the word **leader** in the title, which felt emotionally important at the time.

The job paid slightly more than minimum wage.

Every morning, I picked up a van full of teenagers—many of them gang-affiliated—and hauled water, tools, and lunches to whatever work site we'd been assigned. Blackberry abatement. Creek cleaning. One memorable week, we shoveled sand at the beach, which felt uncomfortably on-the-nose given the state of my life at that moment.

I went into that job terrified. I was wildly underqualified in every way that mattered and painfully overqualified in ways that didn't. Still, I showed up.

And something surprising happened.

Those kids had joy.

Not performative joy. Not motivational-poster joy. Real, unfiltered joy. For many of them, this was their first paying job. They were **thrilled** to be working. They talked about their paychecks with reverence. They planned how they were going to spend the "extra" money. They took pride in being tired at the end of the day.

They weren't dreaming of corner offices, exits, or personal brands. They were joyful because they were useful. Because they were earning. Because someone trusted them with real work.

What I learned during that season is that there is joy in the work itself. Not in the title. Not in the prestige. Not even in the pay. There is joy in contributing, in showing up, in doing something that matters to someone—even if that someone is just a stretch of overgrown creek that looks better when you leave than when you arrived.

Leadership, it turns out, is leadership whether you're running a major organization or driving a van full of teenagers to their first summer job. Dignity doesn't come from what you're paid—it comes from being seen and from seeing yourself as capable.

That job didn't advance my career in any traditional sense.

But it quietly restored my faith in work.

FINDING MEANING IN THE MUNDANE

Not all joyful work comes with a dramatic backstory.

Some of it looks like clogged toilets.

For the last fifteen to twenty years, much of my professional life has been spent in commercial real estate—specifically, property management for office buildings. I collect rent, budget expenses, and maintain properties. On paper, it doesn't exactly scream **soul work**. People are too hot or too cold. Something is leaking. Something smells weird.

It would be easy to dismiss this work as mundane. I've certainly tried.

But over time, I discovered something unexpected: meaning isn't assigned by the job description. It's claimed by the person doing the work.

I started asking myself a simple question: **What does this work support?**

What happens because I show up and do it well?

One of the buildings I managed was a medical office building. People came there sick, scared, hopeful, and vulnerable. Doctors healed. Nurses comforted. Families waited. And my role—quiet, invisible, profoundly unglamorous—was to ensure the building didn't add to anyone's suffering.

That the doors opened easily.

That the bathrooms were clean.

That the elevators worked.

That the lights came on.

In my own small way, I was part of the healing.

Our company also focused on sustainability, which added another layer of meaning. Over time, we saved more than **30 million gallons of water**, diverted **3.3 million pounds of carbon** from the atmosphere, and helped our clients save over **a million dollars in energy costs**.

None of that required a corner office or a dramatic speech.

It required paying attention.

There is real joy in knowing that the work you do—no matter how ordinary it may look from the outside—makes the world a little more livable for someone else. That your effort supports health, dignity, and sustainability, or simply helps each day go a little more smoothly than it might have otherwise.

If I were to die tomorrow, I wouldn't be proud of the titles I held or the meetings I led.

I'd be proud that I showed up.

That I made things work.

That I helped—quietly, consistently, without needing applause.

Turns out, that's a pretty good way to live.

If you're reading this and thinking your work doesn't count—because it isn't glamorous, world-changing, or something you'd put on a billboard—I want to gently suggest otherwise. Joy doesn't require a passion project or a perfect title. It shows up wherever care does. Wherever attention does. Wherever someone decides to do the thing in front of them with integrity and a little heart. Even if that thing is fixing a leaky faucet, answering an email, or making sure the lights come on for someone who really needs them that day.

That's work worth doing. It's more than enough.

CHAPTER FIVE

Joy As a Form of Protest

"If we laugh and sing a little as we fight the good fight of freedom, it makes it all go easier."
~ Sojourner Truth

There's a popular assumption that protest has to look a certain way. Serious. Loud. Angry.

That has never been my style.

Not because I don't care or don't understand what's at stake, but because I've learned through experience, not theory, that joy is one of the most effective forms of resistance we have.

Joy disrupts expectations. It refuses to cooperate with fear. It makes cruelty uncomfortable. It's hard to demonize someone who is smiling at you, waving, and standing firmly in their truth. Joy doesn't ask permission, and it certainly doesn't wait for ideal conditions.

Especially in dark times, joy is not frivolous. It is strategic.

This chapter isn't about minimizing pain or pretending that injustice doesn't exist. It's about choosing how we show up in the face of it. It's about refusing to let anger be our only language.

I protest with joy, not because I am naïve but because I am paying attention.

THE STROLLER

Before I ever chose joy as a form of protest, it had already chosen me.

When I was very small—a toddler—I was pushed through a Black neighborhood in a stroller while my mother registered people to vote. I didn't understand what voting meant, why it mattered, or why some people were watching us so closely.

I remember sitting there, being pushed along, watching people sitting on stoops and standing on corners. I remember waving. Smiling. Blowing kisses. Saying hi to anyone who looked my way—as I had just recently learned to do.

My mother moved through that neighborhood with a clipboard and a stroller—an extraordinarily savvy combination, as it turned out. People are far less suspicious of a white woman with paperwork when she was accompanied by a small child enthusiastically greeting everyone as if she was already campaigning for president.

Only later did I realize that what looked like innocence was also strategy.

And what felt like play was, in fact, practice.

These days, I find myself exercising my First Amendment rights more often than I ever expected to at this stage in my life.

And to my surprise, it has been—of all things—**joyful**.

I show up smiling. I wave. I blow kisses. I am often teased for protesting, as if I were the queen of a homecoming parade.

It's not accidental.

Usually, the response is warm and positive—waves back, smiles, honks, laughs. Sometimes it's outright disdain. I've had epithets hurled at me. I've been told to go home, shut up, calm down, be quiet, and be serious.

My response, more often than not, is:

"I'm out here protesting for *your* rights, too."

That usually short-circuits things just long enough to remind everyone—including me—that this isn't about winning an argument. It's about refusing to surrender our humanity.

Not everyone agrees with my approach. In fact, I received an email from a leader in the protest movement I'm currently participating in that stopped me in my tracks—not because it was cruel, but because it revealed something important.

He wrote:

> *"I would like us to think more about what we communicate by our outward appearance and behavior. Fascism is a serious threat and I feel we need to communicate that in our body language. I think talking, waving, laughing don't do justice to the seriousness of the moment. Let's try on 'somber' next time."*

I sat with that for a bit. And then I replied:

> *"I disagree. I prefer to fight hate with love and misery with joy. We are on the same side and you have all of my support, but if my smiles and laughter and blowing kisses are not welcome, I will find another way."*

That exchange clarified something for me.

This isn't about denying the seriousness of the moment. I know exactly how serious it is. But I also know I have lived through enough grief, trauma, and fear to recognize what happens when we let darkness dictate our posture.

I refuse to let it.

At one protest, I shared the story of my mother pushing me through that Black neighborhood while registering voters—how joy, friendliness, and a waving toddler weren't just niceties but strategy. A fellow protester listened quietly and then said, "Your mother would be proud of you."

And I surprised myself by thinking, *Nope.*

Fuck that!

I want **my** daughter to be proud of me.

She's the one I do this for. She's the one I wave for. She's whom I refuse to harden for.

Because the truth is, joy isn't naïveté. It's defiance.

In the darkest and most difficult of times, when cruelty feels ascendant and suffering is everywhere, it's worth remembering that this mess is entirely human-made. Fear. Greed. Power grabs. Money that isn't even real.

Joy, on the other hand, is free.

It's our birthright.

And perhaps best of all, it absolutely infuriates oppressors!

History bears this out. Enslaved people did not lose their joy; in many ways, they wielded it more fiercely than their enslavers. Jewish humor survived Pharaohs, pogroms, and genocide. Black music survived four hundred years of brutality and still taught the world how to dance.

Once, in a very politically incorrect, multi-racial conversation, I blurted out:

"Humor is to the Jews what music is to Black people."

It's a gross generalization—and also a deeply human truth. Both are joy as resistance. Joy as memory. Joy as refusal.

We protest with joy for those who cannot.

We protest with joy for the times when we might wish we had.

If all our worst fears come true tomorrow, we will wish we had enjoyed today more.

So, yes, I smile.

I wave.

I blow kisses.

Not because I don't understand the seriousness of the moment.

But because I do.

And because somewhere deep in my body, this is muscle memory.

And because joy—lived out loud—remains one of the most powerful forms of protest we have.

You don't have to wave or blow kisses if that's not your style. You don't even have to smile.

But if you can find one small way to keep your joy intact while standing for what matters, I promise, it counts. And it might just be what keeps you going when everything else feels heavy.

CHAPTER SIX

Joy of Nature

"There is something infinitely healing in the repeated refrains of nature—the assurance that dawn comes after night and spring after winter."
~ Mary Oliver

One of the things I find most joyful about nature is that it reminds me I am not important.

And I am not unimportant, either.

I am just another Earth creature.

That might sound dismissive at first, but it isn't. It's clarifying. Comforting, even. Nature doesn't care what I do for a living, how productive I've been, whether I've made good choices, or if I'm in the middle of a personal growth arc. It doesn't track my achievements or judge my failures. It doesn't need my permission, approval, or understanding.

The ocean will roll in whether I'm ready or not. The fog will settle wherever it pleases. The ground will move when it decides to. Nature doesn't perform for us, explain itself to us, or soften its edges to make us feel safer.

And somehow, instead of making me feel small, that makes me feel held.

In nature, I'm relieved of the exhausting job of being the center of the story. I don't have to fix anything, prove anything, or optimize anything. I can just exist—breathing, observing, responding—like every other living thing on this planet has done for far longer than I've been here.

Joy, in nature, doesn't come from being special.

It comes from belonging.

OCEAN, SCALE, AND PERSPECTIVE

The ocean is very good at reminding you who is in charge.

I have spent a fair amount of time in and around it—swimming, snorkeling, paddling, sailing, and standing at its edge to enjoy the view. The message is always the same: *you are welcome here, but you are not running this show.*

The water can be impossibly beautiful—clear, blue, and inviting—and at the exact same time powerful, dangerous, and entirely indifferent to your plans. It doesn't care how strong you think you are, how good your intentions are, or how expensive your swimsuit was.

Swimming off the coast of Santorini—and yes, I know it is a sea and not an ocean, but it still counts—I was overwhelmed by how clear, blue, immense, and powerful it was. I love this planet! Thank you, Earth! Thank you, God!

There is something profoundly humbling about being immersed in something that existed long before you and will continue long after you're gone. Floating in the ocean, I often feel small and insignificant—strangely, deeply loved at the same time. Supported. Held up. Carried.

Nature has a way of stripping away our illusions of control without being cruel. It doesn't shame us for our smallness. It simply reveals it. In doing so, it gives us permission to rest.

When I'm in the water, I don't think about productivity, success, or whether I'm doing life "right." I think about breathing. About balance. About staying upright and not swallowing saltwater like an amateur.

And that's enough.

Joy shows up there not as excitement or accomplishment but as presence. As awe. As the quiet relief of realizing that the weight of the world does not, in fact, rest on my shoulders—and never did.

SHARKS (OR RESPECT IS NOT OPTIONAL)

At some point, awe tips into humility's more assertive cousin, fear.

Once in Hawaii, my husband and I signed up for an excursion called *Swim with Sharks*. It sounded adventurous and empowering, and like something that would make an excellent photo for the Christmas card. The brochure featured smiling people in swimsuits, which should have been my first clue.

The plan was to take a boat out into the open ocean and lower us into a shark cage. A cage, we were assured, was perfectly safe.

I was initially skeptical because we had been on a dolphin cruise the day before and had not seen a single dolphin. I shared this with our shark crew, and they assured me that today would be different. Everything felt fine until we were far enough out that our guide—Bubba, because of course his name was Bubba—began chumming the water. That's when we stood up and saw fins heading toward us from every direction.

Bubba cheerfully explained that they come to this exact spot every day to chum the water. The sharks know they are coming and hear the boat's engine the way we hear a dinner bell.

That was my second clue.

The cage turned out to be… aspirational. It was open at the top and the bottom. Once I was in the water, surrounded by sharks, it became clear there was no meaningful barrier between us and them. This was not a *human—animal connection* moment. This was not a *spirit animal* experience.

We were snacks.

I remembered hearing that sharks don't like the taste of humans, which is comforting until you realize that tasting is involved.

Being there stripped away any illusion that nature exists for our entertainment. We were not guests of honor. We were not special. We were meat floating in someone else's kitchen.

After our small group was pulled back onto the boat—alive, shaken, and newly respectful—another small group took our place. The next group included several beautiful young women, with whom Bubba had been flirting while we faced certain death in the open ocean. Bubba, apparently forgetting the lesson he had just helped teach us, decided to impress them.

He jumped in.

Immediately, the sharks swarmed him. He began punching them in the nose, yelling, diving under the water, and coming up into the cage screaming, "REEL US IN!"

All flirtation not only ceased but was completely forgotten. We did manage to get everyone in the cage reeled in safely.

Once Bubba was safely back on the boat—white as a sheet and shaking like a leaf—his crewmates scolded him for "going in hot." Apparently, if you're going to jump into chummed waters full of sharks, there is a *right way* to do it, and Bubba had not done it.

They then begged us not to tell anyone because they weren't supposed to do that.

Oops. First of all, thank God this episode did not end in tragedy... and it easily could have. It would have been a long, silent boat ride back to shore and a very different kind of vacation after that. Secondly, of course, I'm going to tell everybody! This is a great story!

Everyone survived. No sharks were harmed. Bubba learned nothing.

But I learned a great deal.

Nature doesn't care whether you're brave or foolish. It doesn't respond to confidence or charm. It responds to reality. To respect. To understanding where you stand in the food chain.

Joy, I realized, isn't about conquering nature or proving yourself in it. It's about knowing when you're small, acting accordingly, and being grateful to live to tell the story.

Preferably without becoming lunch.

NATURE AS PERSPECTIVE

As you know, I have been privileged in my later years to enjoy international travel. Traveling the Mediterranean has been more than luxurious.

It has been enlightening, perspective-building, humbling, and hopeful.

Standing at the intersection of Europe, Asia, and Africa—of Islam, Christianity, and Judaism—of history and the future, while also being held by earth, sea, and sky, has been a profound experience for me.

Nature doesn't separate these things as we do.

The land doesn't care which stories we tell ourselves about ownership, borders, or righteousness. The sea doesn't pick sides. The sky covers everyone.

I try to carry that with me now—not just when I'm traveling but at home. To live with curiosity instead of judgment. Amusement instead of frustration. Joy instead of despair.

Not because the world is simple.

But because it's vast.

One of the things I find most joyful about nature is that it reminds me I am neither important nor unimportant.

Sometimes I'm just another Earth creature.

The ocean doesn't need my opinion. The sharks don't care about my résumé. The sky doesn't pause just because I'm having a moment.

Nature isn't impressed by us, but it doesn't reject us either. It simply keeps going—breathing, moving, and offering beauty and danger in equal measure.

When I remember that, I don't feel diminished.

I feel relieved.

I belong here. Not at the center of things—but inside them. And that's a joyful place to be.

PART III

Seeing Clearly

CHAPTER SEVEN

Joy vs. Privilege

"Privilege is when you think something isn't a problem because it's not a problem to you."
~ Unknown

One of the perks of privilege is that you don't even notice it.

I didn't grow up thinking of myself as particularly advantaged. I wasn't wealthy. I wasn't powerful. I wasn't insulated from pain, confusion, or fear. What I was, however, was able to move through the world without constantly having to account for how I might be perceived—or punished—for simply existing.

That distinction took me a long time to understand. I didn't learn it from books, panels, or statistics. I learned it from moments so small they barely registered at the time. Moments that only revealed their meaning decades later, when you finally understood what you did *not* have to notice.

THE THINGS I DIDN'T KNOW I WASN'T SEEING

When I was a small child, I was part of one of the earliest voluntary school desegregation programs. I was bused to a kindergarten in a Black neighborhood. I didn't realize it was unusual or controversial. I just knew I was going to kindergarten. I didn't even notice I was a white kid in a mostly Black school.

I remember two things very clearly.

The first is jump rope.

Those girls could jump rope like it was a sacred art form. Double Dutch. Fancy footwork. Rhythms and patterns that felt like magic. I didn't own a jump rope. I lived alone with my single working mother. I had never learned. No one had taught me.

I would stand there, waiting for my turn, watching in awe. When I finally jumped in, I would be immediately whipped by the rope and sent back out, defeated and vaguely confused. It's funny now. At the time, it just felt like another place where I didn't quite know the rules—but no one ever made me feel unsafe for not knowing them.

The second memory stayed with me longer.

I was playing cards with another little girl. She was cheating. I knew she was cheating because I was, even then, a terrible liar and an excellent tattletale. I told her I was going to tell the teacher.

She looked at me and said,

"I ain't afraid of no white patty."

I had never heard that phrase before. I assumed she thought my name was Patty.

"My name's not Patty," I said, helpfully. "It's Carolyn."

And she walked away.

That was the end of it.

No punishment. No follow-up. No danger. Just a moment that passed.

It wasn't until much later that I understood what had actually happened. She hadn't been misnaming me—she had been naming something *else*. Something I didn't yet know I carried. Something I didn't yet understand meant protection.

One morning, not long after I started kindergarten, I was riding the bus with my older friends. I was having so much fun that I got off the bus when they did. Moments later, the bell rang, and they all went inside. That was when I realized the awful truth. I had gotten off at the wrong stop.

I was very small. Small enough that this felt less like a mistake and more like a catastrophe. I stood there with my backpack and lunch; absolutely certain I had ruined everything. Being the independent young woman that I was, I immediately broke down in tears at the curb.

A Black man noticed me standing there. I was clearly confused, distraught, and very out of place. He asked where I was supposed to be going. I told him the name of my school.

He paused, looked at me for a moment, then said, "Come on. I'll take you."

I got into his car.

Let me say that again, slowly, because it matters:

I got into a stranger's car. Without fear. Without hesitation. Without consequence.

He drove me to school, walked me inside, and made sure I was safe before he left.

Later, I learned who he was. He wasn't just a kind stranger. He was the school board chairman.

At the time, I didn't understand how extraordinary it was. I only knew I had been helped. An adult had noticed me. Nothing bad had happened.

What I understand now is something else entirely.

I was protected in ways I didn't earn and didn't see. I moved through the world, buffered by assumptions of innocence and safety that were never extended equally. A Black child standing alone at the wrong bus stop may not have been offered the same ride and probably would have known not to take it. The Black man who offered me the ride knew he was taking a serious risk, but my comfort and safety took precedence over his own.

This wasn't just kindness.

It was kindness *plus* privilege.

I carried that invisible protection with me for years before I learned to name it.

WHAT PRIVILEGE ACTUALLY LOOKS LIKE

What strikes me now isn't guilt. It's clarity.

I wasn't targeted.

I wasn't watched.

I wasn't assumed to be dangerous, dishonest, or disposable.

I could be bad at jump rope.

I could misunderstand an insult.

I could tattle and walk away unscathed.

That's privilege.

Not comfort. Not ease. Not happiness.

Just the freedom to be awkward, ignorant, and wrong—without consequences.

THE MOMENT IT FINALLY CLICKED

Years later, I began to notice something else.

In rooms full of people—at events, gatherings, and meetings—people of color often seek one another out. A nod. A glance. A moment of recognition.

I realized I was doing the same thing, looking for people of color in every crowd.

And then I realized something else.

They weren't looking for me.

Not because I wasn't welcome.

Because I wasn't necessary for their safety.

That's when I understood: I move through the world *seeking connection*. Others move through it *seeking awareness*.

And that difference?

That's the part you don't see when you're privileged.

SEEING WHAT I WASN'T REQUIRED TO SEE

Recently, I was contacted by a young man writing his doctoral thesis on that early desegregation program. He invited me to participate in a panel and attend a screening of a documentary made at the time, *The Mood of America*, produced by the BBC.

I hadn't known the film existed. Apparently, it was difficult to find and had never been aired. This was one of the first public screenings in over fifty years.

Watching it was... unsettling.

The film itself was extremely dated and full of implicit bias. I could feel the whole audience squirming at the sight of mothers casually smoking cigarettes while being interviewed, and at the filmmakers' obvious contempt for our beloved artist (read Hippie) culture.

The film showed open hostility, racial rage, fear, and violence swirling around the very program I remembered as mostly joyful and foundational. Parents screaming. Communities torn apart. Adults terrified of what change represented.

And there I was, watching it as someone who had lived *inside* that moment—yet had experienced none of that fear.

That's when it landed again.

One of the most profound privileges of privilege is that you don't have to recognize your own privilege.

As a child, I experienced the program as safe, loving, even magical. I learned early that classrooms could be diverse, and that friendships crossed lines adults seemed obsessed with drawing. I remember teachers who were kind, rigorous, and invested in us. I remember feeling lucky. I still feel lucky to have had that experience.

What I did **not** experience was the danger surrounding me.

What I did **not** carry was fear.

What I did **not** have to manage was the emotional cost of being someone else's political experiment.

That invisibility?

That was my privilege.

THE QUESTION THAT STILL HAUNTS ME

As the panel discussion began, I looked around the room and realized something else.

I was the only former student present.

There were Black teachers from that program.

There were scholars.

There were community members.

But none of the Black students I remembered—the kids whose names and faces I still carry—were present in the room.

And my first question wasn't academic or philosophical. It was heartbreakingly simple.

Where are they?

I don't know the answer to that question.

But I know why I was there—and why they may not have been.

WHAT I CARRY FORWARD

Privilege doesn't mean your life was easy.

It means some things were easier *than you knew*.

It means you've got to remember the joy without paying the price.

It means the danger happened *around* you, not *to* you.

And once you see that—once you really see it—you can't unsee it.

The work, then, is not shame.

The work is a responsibility.

To listen more than you speak.

To notice who is missing from the room.

To use the joy you were given not as insulation but as fuel.

Somewhere in the middle of all this reckoning, I had the absurd thought:

Well, at least I was bad at jump rope.

It felt important to remember that the child I was didn't wake up in the morning thinking, *Ah yes, today I will experience structural privilege.* I was mostly thinking about snacks, recess, and whether I would get clobbered by a rope again.

Awareness comes later. Sometimes much later. And sometimes it arrives wearing academic jargon and a BBC logo, which feels unnecessarily formal for a realization that ultimately lands right in the gut.

That realization—that wanting connection and needing protection are not the same—followed me into adulthood.

I've always been most comfortable in diverse spaces. I seek them out instinctively. So, years later, when I found myself struggling to fit in at a small, conservative college, it made perfect sense to me to move off campus into the Black Student Union house when a room opened up.

I thought I'd found home.

What I didn't understand yet was that *comfort* and *belonging* are not interchangeable. That you can feel aligned with a community's values and still not be part of its lived reality. That proximity does not erase difference. And that, even with the best intentions, you remain an outsider.

I didn't experience hostility so much as distance. Parties I wasn't invited to. Conversations that stopped when I walked into the room. The unmistakable sense that my presence changed the temperature, even if no one could quite say why.

Privilege doesn't mean you never feel awkward, rejected, or out of place.

It means those moments don't carry the same risks.

Once you start to see that, the question stops being *Where do I belong?*

It becomes *Who am I making room for?*

Joy, when paired with awareness, becomes something generous.

Something shared.

Something that can widen the circle instead of guarding the gate.

And honestly? That's the kind of joy I'm interested in now.

CHAPTER EIGHT

Joy as a Form of Faith

"I am a bold, brilliant, beautiful creation of a God that loves me."
~ Carolyn Pistone

For a long time, I thought faith was something you either had or didn't—like a membership card or a list of rules you memorized and hoped you got right. Instead, what I've come to understand is that faith lives much closer to the body than the brain. It shows up in how we get out of bed, how we treat ourselves when we fall short, and how we keep choosing love when fear would be easier.

For me, joy isn't separate from faith; it's evidence of it. Not the loud, performative kind, and not the denial-of-reality kind either. Just the steady, stubborn knowing that I am here on purpose, that I am loved, and that this life—messy, miraculous, unfinished—is worth showing up for with my whole heart.

We are not put on this earth to be a good daughter, sister, wife, mother, or a good citizen.

We are not here to earn our worth through service, sacrifice, or obedience.

We are entitled to love, to joy, to pleasure, to rest, to curiosity, and to wonder—because this life and this planet are ours too. Not as a reward. Not as something we qualify for.

But because we are part of it.

Because we exist.

Because we are already love.

When I first adopted my foster daughter, she was four and a half years old and absolutely a hell on wheels.

One morning, after what felt like the tenth time-out before breakfast, we were both on the couch—because, at that point, Mom needed a time-out, too. (I had clearly lost control of the situation.)

She leaned over, patted my thigh, and said calmly,

"You know, Mom, before I was with you and I was all those other places, I knew you were out there."

I just sat there on the time-out couch, spiritually outmatched by a preschooler!

This tiny human had been adrift in the world—shuttled from place to place, from adult to adult—yet somewhere deep inside herself, she carried a certainty that a mother existed for her. That love was real. That it was coming.

That kind of faith has probably saved her life a thousand times since.

And honestly? It saved mine, too.

Earlier in my life, I was hospitalized with Guillain-Barré syndrome—unable to walk and struggling to feed and dress myself—I was overwhelmed not only by fear but by how suddenly small my world had become.

I had just moved to a new town and started at a new school. I barely knew anyone.

And yet people showed up.

Classmates and teachers visited me in the hospital. They brought food to my husband, kept me up to date on schoolwork, and prayed for me.

This is the part that caught me completely off guard.

I didn't have much of a relationship with God at the time, but these people did. And they used it... on me.

I remember thinking, almost incredulously:

You had a chance to talk to God. And you talked to God about ***me***?

That felt like a kind of love I didn't know how to earn and hadn't thought to ask for.

And then—just as suddenly as they had appeared—many of those people faded out of my life once I recovered. That made it even clearer to me that they were there for a reason, for a season. Angels sent to walk me through the hardest stretch, then quietly released back into the world.

Faith, I learned, doesn't always come with answers. Sometimes it brings casseroles, prayers, and borrowed strength.

There was another time when I was struggling financially in ways that were both very real and very private.

Outwardly, everything looked fine. I was running my business. I was active in the community. I was doing what we so often do—holding it together in public while quietly praying the math would work out in private.

It was December when another businesswoman in my community came to see me. She handed me a check and said simply,

"Carolyn, I'm giving you this as my form of tithing—for all you do for our community and for the planet."

I burst into tears.

She had no idea how desperately I needed that money. None. She wasn't rescuing me. She wasn't swooping in. She was just listening to something in her own soul for her own reasons and responding to it.

That check got me through a very hard moment. More than that, it reminded me I wasn't alone—even when it felt like I was doing everything all by myself.

Years later, I found myself on the other side of that exchange.

I went to hear a woman speak—an empowerment speaker—

someone who had unknowingly made a difference in my life simply by telling the truth about hers. My daughter came with me. As she spoke, I realized that parts of her story mirrored some of the hardest things my daughter had lived through.

Afterward, I felt the same quiet nudge I had once benefited from.

So, I sent her a check. Not anonymously, but unexpectedly. It was my own form of tithing.

It turned out to be exactly what she needed at that moment. It carried her through what had been—unknown to me—a very difficult stretch in her life.

I don't think this was a coincidence. I don't think it was magic, either.

I think we're all walking around as potential angels, bumping into one another at just the right moment. I think God—or love, or grace, or whatever name you use—moves through us when we're willing to listen and act.

And sometimes faith doesn't look like belief at all.

Sometimes it looks like a check written at the right time.

Sometimes it looks like receiving one—and letting yourself be helped.

Sometimes, much later, you realize you were part of something sacred... even though at the time you were just trying to make it through December.

I like to say I have spent my life dining at the spiritual buffet. I have dabbled in Christianity, Judaism, paganism, and briefly Tibetan Buddhism. During my Buddhist phase, I met regularly with a meditation group. In one session, we were guided through a beautiful forest meadow and invited to imagine a glowing tree.

We were to approach the tree, notice a hole in it, and reach into the hole, where we would find a special gift just for us. In my mind, I stood on my tiptoes and reached into the hole. My fingers touched... nothing.

I began frantically feeling around in there as if I'd lost a contact lens. Nothing. Afterward, we all discussed what we'd received. One got a beautiful diamond, another a special flower, and another a feeling of lasting warmth and peace.

When it was my turn, I answered honestly. There was nothing in the tree for me. The meditation guide looked at me for a moment, then said matter-of-factly, “You have a problem receiving.” She moved on to the next person.

I was floored! She was right! I have spent the years since that day reminding myself to accept all the gifts this life offers. I guess that was the gift in that tree after all.

I don’t think faith is about being good enough, certain enough, or spiritual enough.

I think faith is what shows up when we trust that love is already in motion—sometimes before we are, and sometimes long after we doubt it.

It’s the child who knows her mother exists somewhere.

The prayers we didn’t ask for but needed.

The check that arrives at the wrong or right moment.

The gift offered by a glowing tree.

If you’ve ever wondered whether you’re being held—even when you’re unsure of what you believe—I suspect the answer is yes.

Sometimes, just to keep things humble, that faith arrives disguised as a kid on the time-out couch, patting your leg and telling you she always knew you were out there.

For me, faith is no longer about belief systems or doctrines. It’s about trust.

Trusting that joy is not frivolous.

Trusting that love is not naïve.

Trusting that kindness matters—even when it doesn’t win.

Faith is believing we are already worthy of love, joy, and belonging—not because we’ve earned it, but because we exist. Because we are part of this beautiful, messy, and miraculous life.

If joy has found you—even briefly—trust it.

It may be faith trying to get your attention.

And it has surprisingly good timing.

CHAPTER NINE

Tick Tock: Joy, Love, & Mortality

"The trouble is, you think you have time."
~ often attributed to Buddha

"If all of our worst fears come true tomorrow, we will wish we had enjoyed today more."
~ Carolyn Pistone

I have spent a good portion of my life treating time as a ubiquitous and renewable resource. Something I could borrow from tomorrow if I needed to. Something that would wait patiently while I handled the urgent, the responsible, and the expected. I assumed there would always be more time to say the thing, take the trip, mend the rift, fall in love harder, or forgive myself later.

Of course, that's nonsense.

Time is not cruel, but it is deeply indifferent. It does not slow down because we're busy, scared, or still figuring things out. It keeps moving—quietly and steadily—whether we are paying attention or not. Then, sooner or later, every one of us is forced to confront the same uncomfortable truth: None of us knows how much of it we actually have.

This chapter isn't about death in a dark or morbid way. It's about what becomes possible once we stop pretending we're exempt from it. When you truly accept that the clock is ticking—loudly or softly, quickly or slowly—you don't necessarily become more fearful.

You become more awake.

You love with greater urgency. You waste less time on nonsense. You laugh more easily. You forgive faster. You say yes when your instinct says yes and no when your soul is tired. You stop saving joy for a future that isn't guaranteed and start spending it in the only place it's ever been available: Right here. Right now.

When I was in sixth grade, a boy I went to school with died.

He and a group of his friends had come to school over the weekend and somehow managed to get on the roof—doing the kind of fearless, rule-blind things eleven-year-old boys do when they still believe, deep down, that nothing bad can really happen to them. At some point, he slipped. He fell through a skylight and crashed to his death.

There was no meaning in it. No illness. No long goodbye. No lesson wrapped neatly around the tragedy. One moment he was alive, and the next he wasn't.

Our entire community was stunned. Parents didn't quite know what to say to their children. Teachers seemed shaken in a way I hadn't seen before. Even at that age, I remember sensing that something had shifted—an invisible line had been crossed.

That year, he was commemorated in our school yearbook. Beneath his photo was an anonymous haiku that has stayed with me:

I have always known
that at last I would take this road,
but yesterday I did not know
that it was going to be today.

I didn't have the words for it then, but I do now. That haiku says everything this chapter is about.

We all know—intellectually—that this road exists. That life ends. That time is finite. But most days, we live as if today has been quietly guaranteed. That tomorrow is a given. That the clock is ticking, yes—but not for us. Not yet.

Until one day, it is.

That was the first time I understood—not fully, but enough—that mortality is not just something that happens to other people. It's not reserved for the old, the sick, or the unlucky. It's woven into the fabric of being alive, whether we acknowledge it or not.

And once you've seen that—even once—you never quite unsee it again.

A few years later, death returned to my life in a different way—quieter, slower, and somehow just as devastating.

When I was in my sophomore year of high school, one of my friends was dying of cancer. He knew it. We knew it. And yet we were still teenagers, going to school, pretending exams mattered, and acting as if the future was something we could count on.

There was a song he played constantly during that time: **"Seasons in the Sun" by Terry Jacks**. If you're of a certain age, you probably know it. It's a farewell song. A gentle, aching goodbye wrapped in a melody that sounds almost cheerful if you don't listen too closely.

He listened to it over and over while he was dying.

I hadn't heard that song in decades when, one day as an adult, it came on the radio while I was driving to pick up a friend. Out of nowhere. Just like that, I was undone. I couldn't stop crying.

When I got to my friend's house, he climbed into the car, looked at me, and asked, "What's wrong?"

I told him about the song. About my friend. About high school. About cancer. About death showing up way too early.

He didn't rush to comfort me. He didn't try to fix it. He paused, looked at me, and said:

"You're crying because you're alive. And you can."

He was right.

Grief had cracked something open in me—but not in a way that diminished life. In a way that proved it. The pain wasn't evidence of weakness. It was evidence of presence. Of having loved. Of still being here to remember.

We spend so much energy trying not to feel—to numb, distract, and outrun the ache—when the ache itself is sometimes the point. Tears are not a failure of strength. They are a privilege of still being alive.

That moment didn't erase the sadness. It changed my relationship with it. I understood then that grief and gratitude are not opposites. They are companions. You don't get one without the other.

Sometimes, crying isn't about death.

Sometimes, it's about life insisting on being felt.

Later in life, death didn't come as a shock. It arrived slowly and deliberately, with time to prepare.

When my mother was dying, we were in the hospital making arrangements to bring her home to hospice. It was clear she wouldn't live more than a few days. I was sitting quietly in her room when the hospital chaplain came in.

I told him, politely but firmly, that we were not a religious family and that I didn't believe he had anything to offer me.

He didn't argue.

Instead, he said two things I have carried ever since.

First, he told me my mother could still hear me—even though she wasn't responsive. He said hearing is one of the last senses to go.

Then he said that at the end of life, there are only a few things that truly matter to say. He offered them simply, without ceremony:

Thank you for everything you've brought into my life.

I'm sorry—for anything and everything.

Please forgive me.

I forgive you.

That was it.

No theology. No platitudes. Just a small, merciful checklist for leaving nothing important unsaid.

What a beautiful gift he gave me!

Today, as I navigate life with my father in his ninety-ninth year, I've made sure not to save those sentences for some imagined final moment. I say them now—out loud when I can, and always in my heart.

Because none of us knows when the last conversation will be or what the last words will be.

What I do know is this: I don't want to die with a grudge. I don't want to die holding onto resentment or waiting for forgiveness that never came. I want to die grateful. I want to leave only love behind for those who remain.

If time is the great teacher in this chapter, then this may be its clearest lesson: Say the important things while you still can. Don't wait for hospice to give you permission.

Life is fragile. Love is urgent. Gratitude, it turns out, is one of the most generous ways to say goodbye—even while we're still here.

And maybe that's why I've never had much patience for pretending that any of this is theoretical.

When my kids were little and I was being what they considered *excessively* cautious—telling them to look both ways, wear their helmets, buckle their seatbelts, and practice proper bicycle safety—my son would sometimes roll his eyes and say, rather snarkily, "Mom, it's not like anybody's going to die."

And I would smile sweetly and say, "Actually, sweetie, we're all going to die."

He didn't find that comforting.

I did.

Once you accept the clock is real, you stop wasting time pretending otherwise. You love more honestly. You forgive faster. You say the important things sooner. You laugh when you can—especially at yourself.

And you keep going, not out of fear of the ending but out of gratitude for the days that are still ticking.

CHAPTER TEN

Joy, Gaslighting, and the Reclamation of Self

"The most common way people give up their power is by thinking they don't have any."
~ Alice Walker

I have come to realize—almost too late in life—that I wasted years gaslighting myself.

My early life taught me I was unlovable. Shameful. A burden. That love was something to be earned by twisting myself into a pretzel—by becoming whatever someone else wanted me to be.

I learned to prioritize others' happiness, comfort, and whims over my own. I became exquisitely observant—some might say hypervigilant—of others' needs and learned to anticipate them before they were expressed.

That kind of training sticks.

My first husband pushed me to become an actor like him. I have no regrets about my acting career, and I genuinely enjoyed much of what it brought me. But I didn't pursue it out of a deep, burning passion for the craft.

I remember telling a girlfriend at the time, "I'm not afraid my husband will leave me for a better wife. (I'd gotten very good at making him need me.) I'm afraid he'll leave me for a better actress."

I threw myself completely into every job and every romance in order to be worthy of love—only to realize the love I received was false because it wasn't based on who I really was. They loved the performance. Not the person.

Years later—many years later—my current and final husband, whose love is my oxygen, said to me, "Don't you believe I love you?"

Without hesitation, I said, "Oh, I believe you love me. I just think you're wrong."

After many years—nay, decades—of wandering the world seeking validation, I have finally begun to know and love the real me.

I've reconnected with people who knew me *when*—before the over-functioning and the pretzel-twisting. I've discovered all that effort had been completely unnecessary. They knew me for real. They loved me for real.

Recently, I apologized to my ex-husband—yes, we're still close friends; otherwise, we'd have to kill each other because we know too much. (My current husband is fine with this. He calls him his *husband-in-law*.) I apologized for something I'd said years earlier that was mean.

He looked at me and said, "Carolyn, I've known you for over forty years, and you don't have a mean bone in your body."

For reasons I still don't entirely understand that comment filled me with immense gratitude. After everything we'd been through—the good and the bad—what he remembered wasn't my cooking or my carefully curated youthful good looks. Instead, it was something fundamental to my character. I was kind.

Wow.

In my sixties, I've reconnected with friends and lovers from the past and seen clearly that what they loved—and still love—about me has nothing to do with my façade or my exhausting attempts to be all things to all people. They saw the real me. The me who is still here.

Oh, the time and energy I have wasted!

If I could share one freedom with the world, it would be this: *Being enough is enough.*

One last thing about that "I think you're wrong" moment—my husband has loved that belief right out of me. He has also done it in front of my daughter. She is the only other person on earth who loves me the same true way he does.

I believe the best thing a man can do for his children is to love, honor, and cherish their mother.

And yes, I understand how ironic it is that it took me six decades, two marriages, a former husband-in-law, and a small personal reckoning to figure it out.

Growth is slow. Self-awareness is humbling. Apparently, I am a long-form learner.

Here's what makes self-gaslighting especially hard to spot: The world applauds it.

We call it being adaptable. Easygoing. Strong. Generous. Low-maintenance. A team player. We praise people—especially women—who can bend without breaking, absorb discomfort without complaint, and make themselves smaller, softer, or more useful in the name of harmony.

I became very good at this.

I learned early that if I could anticipate what others needed and be flexible, helpful, talented, and pleasant enough, things would go more smoothly. Doors would stay open. Conflict could be avoided. Love might be earned.

And for a long time, it worked.

Being hyper-competent became camouflage. I could shape-shift into whatever role was required and be praised for it. I was rewarded for disappearing gracefully—commended for my resilience, professionalism, and ability to "handle things." I mistook that approval for belonging.

(If there were a gold medal for quietly absorbing nonsense with a pleasant expression, I would have podiumed.)

The problem with this kind of reward system is that it trains you to confuse survival skills with personality traits. What began as a way to stay safe becomes who you think you are. You forget that adaptability was a strategy, not an identity.

And because the world keeps handing out gold stars for it, no one pulls you aside and says, *Hey... you're allowed to take up more space than this.*

Not bosses. Not partners. Not institutions. Often not even friends.

So, you keep going. You keep adjusting. You keep polishing the version of yourself that fits best in the room until one day you realize you've been applauded for a role you never auditioned for, and you're exhausted from the performance.

That's the trick of self-gaslighting: It doesn't feel like betrayal. It feels like success.

At some point, I realized this wasn't just personal.

The same mechanisms that taught me to doubt myself were operating at scale—embedded in our systems, institutions, government, media, and workplaces. The messaging changes, but the effect is familiar: *You're overreacting. This isn't that bad. This is just how things are.*

We are told to accept less—less safety, less dignity, and less agency—while being reassured that it's for our own good. That the problem isn't the system; it's our expectations. That if we're uncomfortable, we must be doing something wrong.

Sound familiar?

We're encouraged to hand over our power in exchange for the illusion of stability. To trade joy for compliance. To confuse exhaustion with responsibility and numbness with maturity. To stay quiet, stay busy, and stay grateful—especially when things aren't working.

And the most effective trick of all? Convincing us that joy is frivolous. Optional. Indulgent. Something to be postponed until conditions improve.

But joy is not a distraction from what's wrong.

Joy is evidence that something *right* still belongs to us.

When we reclaim our joy—our worth, our voice, and our sense of delight—we interrupt the lie that we are powerless. We stop outsourcing our sense of value to systems that were never designed to protect it in the first place.

Joy doesn't make us naïve. It makes us harder to manipulate.

A person who knows their own worth is much harder to gaslight. A person who remembers what joy feels like is less willing to accept a life stripped of meaning. A person who openly claims joy quietly gives others permission to do the same.

This is not selfish.

This is contagious.

Reclaiming joy is an act of self-love, yes—but it's also an act of courage. It says, *I will not participate in my own erasure.* It also says, *I see what you're doing, and I'm opting out.*

When enough of us do that—when we refuse to believe the lie that we are small, replaceable, or unworthy—something shifts.

Because joy, once reclaimed, doesn't stay private.

It radiates.

Just to be clear, reclaiming joy doesn't require a manifesto or a lifestyle overhaul.

Sometimes it looks like laughing when you're "supposed" to be serious. Sometimes it's wearing the bright thing, saying the honest thing, or choosing rest without first earning it. Sometimes it's noticing you feel lighter—instead of interrogating that feeling, you let yourself keep it.

(Which, for those of us trained in self-doubt, can feel downright rebellious.)

Joy doesn't always arrive with fireworks. Often it shows up quietly, taps you on the shoulder, and says, *Hey. You're allowed to be here. You're allowed to feel good.*

And that's usually how you know you're doing it right.

Once you start to recognize gaslighting—internal or external—you can't unsee it.

You notice how often you're encouraged to doubt your own experience. How quickly systems ask you to shrink, comply, be patient, be reasonable, and be grateful for crumbs. How often power depends on convincing people that their exhaustion is normal, their anger inappropriate, and their joy frivolous.

"Baby! Who you gonna believe?
Me? Or your lyin' eyes!"
~ Anonymous Womanizer

Reclaiming your joy interrupts that pattern.

Not in a dramatic, overthrow-the-table kind of way. More like a quiet refusal to abandon yourself any longer. A decision to trust what you feel. To take your own longing seriously. To stop asking for permission to be whole.

This is where joy becomes an act of integrity.

When you choose yourself—your clarity, pleasure, rest, and truth—you are no longer as easy to manipulate. You don't move as predictably. You're harder to scare. Harder to shame. Harder to control.

And here's the part that surprised me most: Choosing yourself doesn't isolate you. It doesn't make you colder or less generous.

It makes you braver.

It gives other people permission to do the same.

When you stop gaslighting yourself, you stop participating in the lie that suffering is a prerequisite for worthiness. You stop modeling self-erasure as a virtue. You stop teaching the next generation that love must be earned by sacrificing the self.

You don't have to announce it. You don't have to convince anyone.

You just live it.

And somehow—mysteriously and beautifully—it becomes contagious.

People notice when you take up space without apology. When you laugh freely. When you rest without guilt. When you say no without explaining. When you say yes because you actually want to.

That's not selfishness.

That's leadership.

And in a world that benefits from your doubt, choosing joy is not just personal healing—it's a quiet, radical reclaiming of power.

So no, I don't have this all figured out.

I still occasionally catch myself apologizing to furniture, second-guessing perfectly reasonable decisions, or wondering whether I'm "allowed" to feel good on a random Tuesday. Old habits die hard. Sometimes they don't die at all—they just nap and wait.

But I'm much quicker now to notice when I've started questioning my own reality rather than trusting it. I'm better at laughing when I catch myself mid-pretzel. And I'm far more willing to say, "Actually, no—I'm good right here."

If reclaiming joy means choosing myself again and again, then fine. I'll keep choosing. Imperfectly. With humor. Occasionally with snacks.

Turns out, being enough is a skill you can practice.

And the more you practice, the quieter the gaslighting gets.

PART IV

Rising

CHAPTER ELEVEN

Joy of Hope

"Hope is a discipline."
~ Mariame Keba

Hope has terrible branding. It is often confused with optimism, positivity, or those aggressively cheerful quotes printed on throw pillows—usually by people who have not recently faced a real crisis.

I don't mean hope like that. I don't mean pretending things aren't broken, smiling through suffering, or insisting that everything will "work out" when we have no evidence it will.

I mean hope as a discipline. A practice. Something you choose, often without enthusiasm, sometimes without energy, and occasionally while rolling your eyes. In this sense, hope isn't a feeling you wait for—it's an action you take after you know better.

BORROWED HOPE

When I talk about the time in my life when I would pretend to run errands so I could drive around and cry, I need to be clear about one thing.

That wasn't just a difficult season for me.

It was devastating for my children.

Things were unraveling financially, yes—but worse than that, the people and systems I had trusted were failing us in ways that felt unsafe, unpredictable, and deeply unfair. I could absorb a lot of pain for myself. Watching it land on my kids was something else entirely.

I would cry in the car because it was the only place where I could fall apart without frightening them.

Then one afternoon, while we were out shopping—during what felt like the longest December of my life—my daughter spotted a Santa hat.

She didn't *ask* for it. She insisted.

I bought it mostly because it was cheap and I didn't have the energy to argue. What I didn't realize was that I was buying a family heirloom.

She wore that Santa hat every day. Not just through December, but through the rest of elementary school. And middle school. Long past the point when such things are considered "appropriate." Long past the point when other kids had opinions.

She didn't care.

The hat stayed.

At the time, I didn't understand what she was doing. I was too busy trying to hold everything together. But looking back, I see it clearly now.

She was keeping hope alive.

Not in a grand, inspirational way. Not with speeches, plans, or reassurances. Just quietly, stubbornly, and joyfully, refusing to let the darkness cancel Christmas.

She believed in Santa with a ferocity that did not match our bank account, our circumstances, or my internal monologue.

And somehow, that belief held the rest of us up.

Years later, that Santa hat came to me. I inherited it—not because it fit, and certainly not because it's flattering—but because it carries something sacred.

It turns out the hat is also wildly effective. I get smiles at the grocery store. Strangers laugh. Even people on serious business Zoom calls visibly relax when Santa appears in the corner of the screen. Apparently, joy looks a lot like permission.

I wear it to remember that when I couldn't generate hope for myself, my child found it for all of us. That hope doesn't always arrive as confidence, optimism, or plans. Sometimes it shows up as a ridiculous red hat worn with total conviction.

Hope, I've learned, is not always something we create.

Sometimes it's something we borrow.

That's the thing about hope—it doesn't usually arrive with certainty. It doesn't come with guarantees, timelines, or proof that everything will be okay.

Hope shows up when things are *not* okay.

It shows up when you're scared for your kids. When the numbers don't work. When the future feels foggy and the past won't stop knocking. Hope isn't a conclusion—it's a decision. A small, stubborn refusal to give up on tomorrow, even when today is doing its absolute worst.

For a long time, I confused hope with optimism. I thought hope meant believing things would turn out well. But optimism is a luxury. Hope is a muscle.

Hope is putting one foot in front of the other when you don't feel brave. Hope is making dinner anyway. Showing up anyway. Wearing the damn Santa hat anyway.

That's the kind of hope I've learned to trust. Not the shiny kind. The practiced kind. The kind that lives alongside fear, grief, and uncertainty yet still insists on staying in the room.

In the middle of what I privately refer to as my *John Grisham phase*—when my work life had veered sharply into intimidation, threats, and the kind of moral tests that don't come with a handbook—I attended a board meeting for a nonprofit I belong to.

I almost didn't go.

I had a thousand reasons not to. My mind was loud, my nerves were fried, and I was carrying worries that felt much bigger than anything we were going to accomplish at that meeting. But I went anyway, mostly because I knew I would feel worse if I didn't.

One of the young men who had benefited from the nonprofit was there that day. He didn't speak much. He didn't need to. He wore a T-shirt that read:

I am my ancestors' wildest dreams.

And just like that, everything inside me woke up.

Here I was, worried about contracts, consequences, reputations, and the possibility of losing everything I had built. And there he was—reminding me of my ancestors. People who crossed oceans with nothing. No money. No education. No guarantees. No safety net. Just hope, grit, and a willingness to risk everything for the possibility of something better… for me.

That shirt stopped me in my tracks.

Not because it minimized what I was facing—but because it reframed it. It reminded me that hope isn't fragile. It's stubborn. It outlives fear. And sometimes it shows up as perspective.

I briefly considered stealing the shirt, but felt that would undermine the message.

Sometimes hope doesn't come from inside you at all. Sometimes it borrows a body, prints itself on a T-shirt, and stands right in front of you until you remember who you come from and what the next possibility is.

At some point, I realized that hope isn't something I wait for anymore.

It's something I practice.

Every December now, I wear that Santa hat—not for nostalgia, not as a costume, but as a small, deliberate act of defiance against despair. I wear it while running errands, standing in line, and logging in to meetings. It still makes people smile. It still softens the air around me.

What surprises me isn't that it works—it's how little effort it takes.

A hat. A grin. A willingness to look a little foolish.

Somewhere along the way, I discovered I enjoy being Santa far more than I ever enjoyed waiting for Santa. There's relief in that. Agency. A quiet joy in realizing you don't have to believe everything will be fine to choose to be kind, playful, or hopeful anyway.

Hope doesn't need grand gestures. It just needs someone willing to carry it into the world—sometimes in red felt, sometimes with a pom-pom, and always with intention.

And if you're wondering where to find hope next, try *being* hope for five minutes and see what happens.

CHAPTER TWELVE

Joy Rising

"Joy is an act of resistance."
~ Toi Derricotte

I used to think joy was something you earned—after healing, learning, suffering, and proving yourself enough. I thought it would arrive as a reward, or maybe as a consolation prize if you survived with grace.

I was wrong.

Joy doesn't wait for permission. It doesn't require approval. It doesn't ask whether your life looks reasonable from the outside. Joy rises—sometimes slowly, sometimes sideways, sometimes laughing at its own terrible timing—but it rises anyway the moment you stop pushing it down.

I didn't set out to write a book about joy.

I set out to survive my own life.

Joy came later—not as a reward, not as a personality trait, and certainly not as a mood. It arrived as a byproduct of telling the truth. Of stopping the performance. Of no longer confusing endurance with worthiness.

For most of my life, I thought joy was something you were either lucky enough to stumble into or earned through discipline. I thought it belonged to people who had easier childhoods, steadier bank accounts, fewer complications, and better knees. I assumed it was fragile—something that disappeared the moment real life showed up.

I was wrong.

Joy didn't vanish in the face of grief, trauma, injustice, illness, or fear. What vanished was my willingness to postpone joy until everything was resolved, until I was healed enough. Forgiven enough. Certain enough. Thin enough. Brave enough. Right enough.

What rose instead was something sturdier.

Joy rose when I stopped waiting for permission—from institutions, partners, culture, and my own inner critic. It rose when I understood that joy isn't optimism. It's orientation. A way of standing in the world that says: *I'm still here. I'm still paying attention. I'm still choosing to live fully.*

This isn't a triumph story in the traditional sense. There's no neat arc. No finish line. No moment when everything clicks into place and stays that way forever. Instead, there's a practice—sometimes clumsy, defiant, and hilarious—of choosing aliveness again and again.

Joy rising doesn't mean pain goes away.

It means pain doesn't get the final word.

If you're reading this hoping for instructions, I don't have any. But if you're reading this wondering whether joy can survive in a world like this—inside a life like yours—I can tell you this:

Joy is already moving.

It's our birthright, our life force, and our reason to connect and soldier on. It may feel invisible, far away, or buried.

But it rises.

If joy were only personal, it wouldn't matter much.

Nice for us, maybe. Comforting. A coping mechanism. Something to enjoy privately and keep to ourselves, like a favorite song or a guilty pleasure.

But joy isn't just internal. It's contagious.

It changes how we show up. How we speak. How we listen. How we refuse to disappear—even when disappearing would be easier, safer, or more socially acceptable.

What I've learned is this: Joy doesn't rise *instead* of responsibility. It rises *into* responsibility.

When we reclaim our joy, we don't drift away from the world—we become more present in it. Less brittle. Less reactive. Less easily manipulated by fear, shame, or exhaustion. Joy steadies us. It widens our peripheral vision. It reminds us that we are more than whatever crisis is currently shouting the loudest.

This matters.

We live in a time that profits from our despair. From our division. From convincing us that we are powerless, isolated, and small. Joy interrupts that narrative—not loudly, not dramatically, but persistently.

Joy says: *I see what's happening. I'm still choosing to live as if I belong here.*

That choice has consequences.

A joyful person is harder to control.

A joyful community is harder to fracture.

A joyful movement is harder to extinguish.

This doesn't mean we bypass grief, ignore injustice, or sugarcoat reality. It means we refuse to let cruelty be the most creative force in the room.

Every time we choose curiosity over contempt, generosity over scarcity, humor over humiliation, and presence over withdrawal, we carry joy forward. Not as an abstraction but as a practice.

You don't have to be fearless to do this. You don't have to be healed. You don't even have to feel particularly joyful on any given day.

You just have to be willing.

Willing to stay.

Willing to look.

Willing to let joy move through you—even imperfectly.

That willingness is enough to begin.

At some point, joy stops being something we chase and becomes something we pass along.

Usually without realizing it. Not through speeches, declarations, or inspirational quotes taped to the fridge. But through how we live, what we tolerate, and what we finally stop apologizing for.

The people watching us—our children, our friends, our communities—aren't learning about joy from what we *say* about it. They're learning from what we model.

From whether we believe we're allowed to take up space. From whether we rest. From whether we laugh through hard seasons. From whether we stay soft in a world that keeps insisting we toughen up and "be realistic."

I think about the moments that shaped me most, and very few involved someone sitting me down to explain how life works. Most involved watching someone live in a way that made something inside me quietly exhale.

Someone who didn't shrink.

Someone who didn't pretend everything was fine.

Someone who chose delight anyway.

Someone who kept their humanity intact—no matter how inconvenient that was.

That's the legacy joy leaves.

Not perfection.

Not productivity.

Not even constant happiness—thank God, because that sounds exhausting.

Permission.

Permission to be fully alive.

Permission to change your mind.

Permission to feel deeply and still keep going.

Permission to love this life—not because it's easy, fair, or orderly, but because it's *yours*.

We don't get to decide how long we're here. We don't get to control most of what happens to us. But we do get to decide what energy we bring into the room while we're here and what we pass on when we leave.

Joy doesn't erase the hard parts of a life well lived.

It illuminates them.

It says, *I was here. I noticed. I loved. I participated.*

If someone someday remembers me—not for what I achieved but for how I made them feel more like themselves, more hopeful, and freer—then that feels like enough.

More than enough.

That's joy rising.

And once it rises, it no longer belongs to us.

(It never really did.)

It keeps moving.

If you finish this and feel a little braver, a little softer, and slightly less interested in behaving, then come sit by me. I'll pour the wine.

Acknowledgments

This book exists because I am surrounded by people who love, challenge, tolerate, feed, argue with, forgive, and occasionally remind me to drink water and go to bed.

First and always, to my husband—my oxygen. You have loved me with a steadiness and generosity that healed parts of me I didn't even know how to name. You believed in me when I didn't believe in myself. You have laughed with me, traveled with me, held me, and never once asked me to be smaller, quieter, or easier. Loving you has been one of the great joys of my life, and being loved by you has made everything else possible.

To my daughter: You are the reason I do this work and the reason I keep choosing joy, even when it would be easier not to. You have taught me more about hope, resilience, humor, and courage than any book ever could. Thank you for forgiving me when I got it wrong, trusting me when I didn't feel trustworthy, and loving me anyway. I am endlessly proud to be your mom.

To my Bliss Sisters and "Real" Sisters—thank you for the gifts you gave knowingly and the lessons you gave unintentionally. You shaped me in ways both visible and invisible, and I carry you with me through every chapter of this book.

To my friends—old, new, lifelong, and those who reappeared after decades as if no time had passed—thank you for seeing me clearly and loving me anyway. Thank you for the laughter, the late-night conversations, the shared outrage, the shared meals, and the shared silence. You remind me of who I am when I forget.

To the people who trusted me with their stories—in prisons, hospitals, boardrooms, protests, kitchens, and quiet conversations—thank you. Your humanity, courage, and humor live on in these pages.

To my colleagues, collaborators, clients, and fellow Earthlings: Thank you for letting me do meaningful work in the world and for believing that business can be ethical, joyful, and planet-saving. Thank you for reminding me that integrity is not theoretical—it's lived daily, imperfectly, and with intention.

To readers—including those who found *Open for Joy* and those who picked up *Joy Rising* without knowing anything about me—thank you for your time, openness, and willingness to consider joy not a luxury but a birthright and a form of resistance. If any part of this book makes you feel seen, braver, or a little less alone, it has done what it came here to do.

And finally, thank you to joy itself—for being stubborn, sneaky, resilient, and impossible to fully extinguish. You keep showing up, even when I reluctantly invite you, and I'm grateful every time you do.

With love, gratitude, and a healthy dose of mischief,

Carolyn

About the Author

Carolyn Pistone is a writer, speaker, entrepreneur, and committed Earthling dedicated to saving the planet—using her real estate license. She is the author of *Open for Joy: A Journey of Healing and Business Success* and has contributed to multiple anthologies exploring resilience, leadership, and transformation. Her work blends lived experience, hard-won wisdom, humor, and a deeply held belief that joy is not a luxury—it's a birthright.

Carolyn is the President and Managing Director of Clear Blue Commercial, where she brings together sustainability, integrity, and business strategy in service of people, communities, and the planet. She has held senior positions in the entertainment, real estate, and high-tech industries, experiences that have shaped her commitment to building supportive, innovative, and collaborative environments where clients, teams, and—yes—even the Earth can thrive.

As a keynote speaker and workshop leader, Carolyn speaks about joy, courage, boundaries, leadership, and living fully in uncertain times. Her talks are deeply human, thought-provoking, and often unexpectedly funny.

She lives, writes, speaks, and occasionally dances her way through life with curiosity, conviction, and a well-earned sense of humor.

Learn more at https://carolynpistone.com

Visit Amazon for *Open for Joy: A Journey of Healing and Business Success* at: https://www.amazon.com/dp/1735025577

www.ingramcontent.com/pod-product-compliance
Lightning Source LLC
LaVergne TN
LVHW010932110826
845149LV00013B/2556
9798994912119